*Work with
What You
Have*

Work with What You Have

WAYS TO CREATIVE AND MEANINGFUL LIVELIHOOD

Deborahann Smith

SHAMBHALA
BOSTON & LONDON
1999

Shambhala Publications, Inc.
Horticultural Hall
300 Massachusetts Avenue
Boston, MA 02115
http://www.shambhala.com

9 8 7 6 5 4 3 2 1

First Edition

Printed in the United States of America

⊗ This edition is printed on acid-free paper that meets the
American National Standards Institute Z39.48 Standard.

Distributed in the United States by Random House, Inc.,
and in Canada by Random House of Canada Ltd

Library of Congress Cataloging-in-Publication Data
Smith, Deborahann,
     Work with what you have: ways to creative and meaningful
livelihood/by Deborahann Smith.—1st ed.
        p.   cm.
     Includes bibliographical references.
     ISBN 1-57062-114-4 (alk. paper)
     1. Vocational guidance.   2. Career development.   I. Title.
HF5381.S62363   1999   98-6839
650.14—dc21   CIP

Contents

Acknowledgments

Like most forms of work, the writing of a book involves community. I would like to especially thank the following people for their support: Hobart Bell, Elizabeth Bethea, Chris Braider, Helen Howe Braider, Merlin Brotzman, Dorothy Cleveland, Jerry Cleveland, Amelie DeBlois, Mark Fishback, Katherine Kahlife, Jesse and Helen Smith, Jesse F. Smith, Sr. (in memoriam), and Alexander Thomas. Also, much gratitude to Shambhala Publications: to my oh-so-patient editors, Dave O'Neal and Kendra Crossen Burroughs; to Jonathan Green for his endless support; and to all of the Shambhala staff for their important behind-the-scenes work that makes a book appear as if by magic.

In deep appreciation of those who gifted their experiences here.

I think it was Jesus who said, "He who does not dance does not know what happens," although it could have come from Buddha, Krishnamurti, Meher Baba, or one of his other spiritual colleagues. Anyway, this book is dedicated to the ones who fandango on their coffee breaks. They know what happens, they know who they are, and they work with what they have.

INTRODUCTION

I LEARNED about work at the same time I learned how to drive a car. The time was the summer before I went to college. The workplace was a field behind the American Legion Post in Ithaca, New York. And the car was a ten-year-old pig-colored Rambler, circa 1964. My employer/instructor was my grandfather, who managed the Legion that year. The task he set before me was threefold: to get a sense of having a job, to flatten the weeds, and to learn the way of the road. Of course the field wasn't exactly a road, and the Rambler wasn't your typical workplace, but my grandfather said you had to start somewhere and it may as well be there. So that was what I did.

My grandfather's instructions were simple: "Here is the accelerator, here is the brake, and here are the keys. Go to it. When you're finished, come back in and I'll give you your spending money"—"spending money" being what he called my pay. He wheeled the jukebox to the back porch on a long extension cord, removed the coin box cover so I could listen to whatever I wanted on just one quarter, and went inside to finish the Legion accounting. Then I drove around and around and around that field, doing my job, learning to drive, and singing to the jukebox at the top of my lungs.

My grandfather had many different kinds of jobs in his lifetime and probably as many cars. He had advice about both, which he offered up at the end of each day along with a frosty lime and Coke. Watch where you're going. Give your all. It's important to be in the driver's seat as much as possible, but learn to be a good passenger, too. Have self-respect. Unless passing, stay on your side of the road.

When he was sure he had my attention, he continued: Maintain your integrity. Be true to yourself, but embrace the wisdoms of those who have come before you. And keep your spirits about you because, although there are always friends and mentors, you are the one who ultimately sees you through.

I thought about these words as I gave my all to every job I did at the Legion that summer. As I peeled potatoes, waited on tables, and washed dishes. As I scoured bathrooms and buffed floors. I thought about them as I drove, as I graduated from the field, learned the highway, and began to find a sense of where I might be going in life—what my grandfather called the way of the road.

I wondered where that road would take me. I knew the first stop, in the fall, was college. But I couldn't decide where to focus my studies; there were so many crossroads running through my mind. I finally narrowed it down to three choices: psychology, entomology, and writing arts. Psychology, because the stories and inner workings of people have always inspired me; entomology, because I am in great awe of the tiny mysteries of the world; and writing, because I had been doing it since I was old enough to put pen to paper. In the end, the drive to write won out (with many psychology and art classes on the side), choosing me as it always had.

The thing about being a writer is that everything is in your job description. Everything is something to write about, whether you are jack-of-all-trades at the American Legion, giving cooking lessons to four-year-olds at a Montessori preschool, or conducting intake interviews in a county jail. A writing teacher once told me, "Write what you know about. Write what you can find out about. This will take you everywhere." I have since extended this wisdom to work in general: work with what you have. Work with what you can learn. Meet as many people in your field—and other fields—as you possibly can. Whatever your livelihood, this can take you to places beyond your wildest imagination.

When I consider the twenty years of my career, I'm amazed at how far I've come. For the first ten years, I had "permanent" positions, mostly writing and design in the publishing field, with a short time out to teach preschool. Then I went freelance and, in conjunction with publishing books and articles, I pieced together a series of projects to make a king-sized quilt of full-time livelihood. This included conducting workshops on alternative livelihood solutions through city extension programs and alternative learning centers and at Radcliffe College; consulting on corporate employment issues; planning national conferences and events; editing; temporary administration work; puppeteering; and floral design. Now I've come full circle, dividing my time between editing at a natural-lifestyles magazine and writing at home.

One of the best aspects of my work is the people I encounter along the way: A Zen master who works as a psychotherapist. A bus driver who is now a diplomat with the foreign service. A destitute single mom who created a successful business through reselling items she found at flea markets. I've met ordinary people being extraordinary in their everyday jobs by finding things to appreciate about their workdays—and bringing much to those around them in the process. I've seen people find their calling and consequently the work they love. There are so many folks out there from all walks of life discovering for themselves how to make work *work*.

This book is about finding ways to creative livelihood. It's about taking your current employment experience and making it meaningful beyond clocking in forty hours a week. Herein are the real-life experiences of individuals who have created their own places in the working world—plus a few of my own.

When I think of my work experiences, several analogies come to mind. Work is like climbing a mountain. It's like getting into an elevator with the most unlikely characters. It's like jail, like hell, like a story, like a dance. Work is like taking a photograph of yourself and watching it develop. Sometimes it even feels a little like a dream. Of course, work is like driving, too: getting into the car and navigating the way of the work road. It's discovering oh-so-many routes, each with different scenery and a different speed limit, each offering something you don't expect.

My wish is that this book will be a road map for your workaday travels, as the experiences that led to it have been mine. Remember to keep your eyes open for the myriad possibilities. May you be in the driver's seat, rambling all the way.

Getting
Inspired

THE BEGINNING IS THE MOST IMPORTANT PART OF THE WORK

WHEN I hear people talk about work, I'm always impressed by how passionate they are. Whether they love or hate their jobs or are bored 1,000 percent out of their workaday minds, many employees are very strong in their feelings. It's like a wild animal begins to stir inside them. Slowly, that animal yawns, opens its eyes, stretches its legs, moves tentatively about. As it becomes fully awake, that animal is anxious to get out in the world. It begins to notice things, and it's ready to express itself about those things. It's ready to roar.

I met a quality control manager whose work brought out the cougar in her, all fangs and claws. With fire in her eyes and venom in her voice, she announced that she hated her job more than all of the crime in New York City. (Now *that's* a lot of passion, I thought.) I spoke with a man whose job was to blast holes in the ground for house foundations. Unlike the quality woman, his job gave him a sense of accomplishment. In fact, it gave him quite a thrill. The very thought of lighting the dynamite blasted him out of bed at four o'clock every morning; he didn't even need an alarm clock, he told me with glee. Personally, I would hate all those flying rocks, all that noise—especially at such a barbaric hour. But he loved it. When he talked about his work, he reminded me of an eagle: he truly soared.

Yes, whatever feeling their passion brings out, people are full of life when it comes to their work. Full of what they like and dislike. Of what they will do differently, even drastically, when they get the money . . . the opportunity . . . the motivation . . . the time. Some have five-year plans. Others have lifelong goals. A few even have their next lives mapped out. (Don't laugh, I've heard this countless times.) "In my next life," a marketing executive once told me, "I intend to have better professional karma. My work will be more meaningful, more creative. I will be top dog at the company instead of underdog. I will have a lot of independence."

Wow, I think. This is really planning ahead. I think it's good to take responsibility for your future, to create a sense of where you are going, where you want to be. It's important to want to grow in your work. But who wants to wait until the next life to get those qualities into your work? Who wants to wait for even one more year? I don't know about you, but I don't have that kind of patience. I want job satisfaction during *this* lifetime. And I want it to begin *right now.*

Plato said, "The beginning is the most important part of the work." I've considered this a lot. I have written it on pink Day-Glo sticky notes and taped them to my computer. I've said it out loud, mantra-style, until the words practically wore a groove in my brain. I've looked at each of my projects, trying to determine where the beginning was. Still, I ponder exactly where the beginning of work begins. Is it Monday morning? Is it the first thought that launches a new project? Is it deeper than this—a passion for life, a generosity of spirit, a connection with God? Is it all of these things—and more?

Of course, there are all kinds of beginnings, ranging from the simplest gesture to the most complex event. They occur on every level of the intellectual and spiritual realms. Also, beginnings mean something different to each individual. For instance, I knew a woman who worked in a Barbie doll factory in the days before automation, and for years her job was to snap on Barbie's head. Day after day, hour after hour, this was her work: snapping on the heads. Nothing more, nothing less. To me, it sounded as awful as beginning the day by lighting sticks of dynamite, but when I asked how she did it, she only smiled. Then she told me that every morning her husband had awakened her with a cup of coffee and a kiss. He had never missed a day in thirty years. They talked about their dreams while she drank her coffee, before they left for work. How could her day be any less than wonderful, she said, when it began with so much love, so much connection?

For her this was the beginning: coffee and a kiss.

Shortly thereafter, I spoke with a man who had been in combat in Vietnam for three years. For weeks at a time he was out in the field, sleeping on the ground, eating on the run, unable to bathe. Still, every morning he made it a point to wash his face and shave. Even in that embattled jungle, a clean, shaven face gave him a sense of well-being. Even in combat, it offered self-respect.

For him this was the beginning: cleanliness and self-respect.

A photojournalist friend once told me she was thirty-seven years old before she realized she actually worked for a living. At that point she had been in the workforce for fifteen years and had photographed just about everything imaginable: two people shaking hands after their cars collided; Buddhist monks creating a sand painting at an art museum; homeless women sleeping beneath a pile of coats; children masquerading at a nursing home as singing frogs. She had taken pictures of rock slides, floods, house fires, blizzardy pro football games, several United States presidents, and the Pope.

All in all, this seemed like a pretty big job to me. But when I asked what she thought of herself as doing all those years, if not working, she replied, "You know, work is just about living my life."

Before this conversation, I had never thought of my job in this way: as simply another activity I did with my life. I had never thought of work as just another element of my human experience.

Yet it made sense in the grand scheme of things. I worked, spent time with family and friends, volunteered at the homeless shelter, cleaned the house, watched spiders spin webs, went to the meditation center. I read, made dinner, made love, walked, went to aerobics class, went to the movies, went to the grocery store. I did all of these things along with my work. Yes, I had a job. And that job was important: it was income, contribution, self-expression, satisfaction. But it worked in complement with the rest of my life. It wasn't really more important than everything else.

Here was another beginning: viewing life as a large picture puzzle—of which work is only a single piece.

Several months ago I saw the Dalai Lama speak. He said, "We all have the potential for happiness in our lives and in our work. As a Buddhist I have found that one's mental attitude is the most influential factor in working toward this happiness. The key is inner peace."

Just as I could see my job on a par with the rest of my life, finding inner peace at the office made sense. But finding inner peace is a very big order. You can't go to the Ideal Market and tumble it into your shopping cart along with the broccoli and lemons and animal crackers. You can't say "Poof!" and make it leap into your head. So where does it come from, inner peace? And how do you get it into your day—especially at work?

In my own life, I have found that focusing on my spiritual center has made a very big difference in my work. Through conscious breathing—what I call Working Meditation—I can catch an occasional glimpse of inner peace. A friend of mine who is a Zen monk says that inner peace comes from paying total attention to whatever he is doing throughout each day. By being fully present in each activity, whether he is sweeping the porch or pulling weeds in the garden, he is able to connect with the quietude of the moment. Another friend finds inner peace through focusing on loving kindness. By getting outside of herself and giving to others—helping, listening—she feels more settled in her work and in her life.

So here is another beginning: finding inner peace.

Okay, maybe the last thing you feel right now is inner peace. Maybe you are more like a grizzly bear that just awoke from a long hibernation, starving and irritable as hell. You hate your job. You hate your boss. Every single one of your colleagues is a clone from hell. You can't imagine finding enjoyable work now, next year, or any time in your next thirty lives. Inner peace? No way. No how.

That's fine. Believe it or not, this is a good place to start. Because there is a lot of energy to work with there. My friend Valerie had a turning point in this area when she had a job cleaning out stables. One day, as she leaned over to scoop some manure, a horse kicked at her, narrowly missing her head. As if this wasn't enough to make her day, the horse then proceeded to produce more manure. Valerie was all curses. She screamed every expletive she had ever heard and coined a few besides. When I mentioned later that she was in touch with her wild animal self, she replied, "No kidding. I was an entire zoo."

But something amazing happened to Valerie then. After the horse failed to respond to her feelings, just continued to chew its hay without apology, Valerie heard herself. She heard in her curses how strongly she felt. She heard how frustrated she was with her work. And in those feelings she suddenly felt energized—and very much alive.

In the next moment Valerie saw many beginnings. A beginning to acknowledge those anger-fueled feelings and use them to move forward. A beginning to realize that although stable cleaning had been the right job for a year, it was time to take charge, to move toward a situation that would fulfill her more. And, as she looked at the manure, she also saw the symbolism: manure as fertilizer to make things grow.

So here is another beginning: using your passions, whatever they are, to take charge of your work and help you grow.

I know, I know. You may wonder how it's possible to take charge when you aren't the boss, when you are definitely not top dog. You may ask, Isn't it up to our companies to be doing more for us, to realize our worth? Shouldn't management be taking charge? In addition, we want appreciation and respect. We want others to fulfill our workaday dreams. But why sit back and wait for this to happen? Why not create our own opportunities, give ourselves what we deserve? After all, we spend 40 percent of our lives at work. Don't we owe it to ourselves to make that time ours, to make our work lives count?

Sometimes the beginning is about finding your open voice and taking responsibility for making your work situation *work*. I recently experienced such a beginning when I found myself in nineteen hours of grueling meetings in one week—which put me behind in my work. I rolled up my sleeves. I was ready to fight for my rights. I expected my editorial director to fight me back. Instead, when I told her I needed to talk, she invited me to a Japanese restaurant for Zen cookies and haiku tea and wanted to know what was on my mind. I blurted out, "I am never going through another week like this in my life." She smiled and replied, "Okay."

WORK TO GET INSPIRED

WHENEVER I want to get inspired in my work, I think of the elephants on the road. This is from a news feature I once heard about a truck driver who was roaring along a familiar highway when another trucker radioed him a warning: "Elephants up ahead!" But the driver didn't believe it. Well, why would he? After all, he had been running this stretch of west Texas highway for half of his life and he had never seen an elephant there before. Armadillos, yes. Rattlesnakes, sure. Javelinas, coyotes, wolves, most definitely. But elephants? No way. Surely, he thought, his colleague was joking—or maybe even hallucinating. There wasn't a chance of elephants. Not on *this* outback Texas road.

Of course, as life in all its unpredictability would have it, it turned out that a circus was camping nearby. From which several elephants had escaped. And yes, Virginia, I mean, er, Texas, they were taking a little highway stroll. Fortunately, the trucker was able to stop in time to believe his eyes. To see that, although they had not been in his previous experiences, there were now indeed elephants on the road.

Sometimes work is like this: traveling the long black highway, driving without event day after day. The centerline pulls you, the rolling hills lull you; you are practically somnambulating as you amble along. You think it could go on like this forever, ho hum, right through this lifetime and into the next. What could possibly happen to make things change?

Then one day, something *does* happen. Maybe it's an elephant. Maybe it's something a colleague says. It might be an idea that strikes you in an unusual way. Whatever it is, because it's different or bizarre, or just because it's in your face, you take a closer look. And suddenly there seems to be more long-range visibility on the road ahead; you see new possibilities on this old familiar route. This is when you feel yourself opening up. You begin to get inspired.

But what is inspiration, really? Is it something divine? Is it something the employment gods sneak in when you least expect it? Is it your subconscious returning to you in "aha!" form the information you have previously gathered and internally processed? Perhaps it is something you go looking for. But then it might be something that just happens, say, an elephant, that lends new perspective to your work. Or possibly it is all of the above: a partnership between our seeking selves and the heavenly muse.

The *Tao Te Ching* says, "When you are open to something, you are one with it, you have access to it." So if you are open to inspiration, it will be accessible to you. Somewhere, somehow, you will find it. Because when you work to get inspired, you are opening up to inspiration's very existence.

I wonder if the truck driver was more open to new experiences in his work after seeing the elephants on the road. I can only guess that maybe he was, although I'm sure he told people about it again and again over the years. I do know, however, that the story inspired me to be more open because now when I sit down to a blank piece of paper, or when I have another project that requires a creative touch, I tell myself, Climb into the semi of your mind. Pay attention as you shift those gears and turn that wheel. Don't limit yourself to your previous experiences; look for some different details in your usual job landscape. Get out into the world and get involved. Because this may be the day something different happens. The day the proverbial elephants appear on the road. And you don't want to miss them when they do.

LISTEN TO YOUR WORK

Around the time I heard about the elephants, I met George Bowman, a Zen master in Cambridge, Massachusetts. Or rather, I should say, I met his voice.

It was a blizzardy February evening. I was sitting on my black meditation cushion in the dim *zendo* (meditation room) and, along with thirty other Zen students, I was following my breath. At least, I assumed the others were following theirs. I was mostly trying to ignore the wrestling match of ideas raging inside my head.

Suddenly George's voice appeared, deep and resonant, dispersing my thoughts and bringing me back into the room. His voice was telling us to listen to the night. "Listen to the night tell its story," was how he phrased it. "*You* don't need to tell the night's story. It isn't necessary for you to think about what it has to say. Listen completely and the night will say its piece."

It's amazing what happens in a room when thirty people are listening. I mean *really listening*, all at once. It's as though they are listening not only for themselves, but for everyone else around them, too. And because of all this listening, everything grows louder, clearer. You can practically hear one another's thoughts.

George was right. As soon as I began to pay attention, the night began to tell its story. There was the clicking of the furnace. Sleet sliding down the windows. The rustling of my neighbor's raw silk pants as she moved ever so slightly against her cushion. I heard a cat meowing softly in another part of the house, a car spinning its wheels in the snow. And the breathing—goodness, all that breathing—in the dark, sweet quiet of the zendo. The night was telling its story, and it had a lot to say.

I thought about this for a long time. Long after I reached the most wonderful tranquillity from my active listening. Long after the night had passed. Years after I came to know the inspiring person beyond George Bowman's voice. I thought, if you can hear the night's story, through listening you can get to the heart of just about anything in your life—including your work.

Of course, unless your work is playing the violin or operating a drill press or listening to a client tell you about his childhood, your work won't exactly make audible sounds. Certainly, when I'm beginning a new writing project, listening doesn't miraculously make my words a book on tape. But I do find that if I listen quietly with complete attention, the words begin to speak from deep inside me in a similar manner. Like watching for the elephants on the road, once I begin to listen, all my senses become activated. I begin to feel what Krishnamurti meant when he said, "In oneself lies the whole world." This is the world of inspiration wherein my work comes alive.

Indeed, many of the world's greatest inspirations have come through listening. A number of important philosophers and painters have come to their ideas through listening to nature. Johann Sebastian Bach used to stay up late, listening to the night. What he heard was all the life questions, all the "what ifs" that wandered through his thoughts. His conclusion was that there would always be more questions than answers, and he wrote his music in response.

One way I listen to my work is by approaching it as a meditation practice. I sit at my desk, or on the floor, and focus for a few minutes on quiet time with my project. I'm not concerned about *doing* the work in this moment. I'm just giving its existence my ear. Sometimes I light incense. Often I sip a cup of herbal tea. Once in a while I add to my cup a few drops of white chestnut Bach Flower Essence, a homeopathic tincture useful for concentration. I continue to sit, watching my thoughts settle and listening to my work.

Once I sat like this for an entire week. I had a writing block I couldn't break, so I listened to my work (and Navajo flute music) and folded origami swans. By the end of the week, I had a thousand swans of different colors and patterns; some were as tiny as ladybugs, some as large as schnauzers. Later, I packed them into a box and sent them off to friends. And my block was thankfully gone.

You don't have to be a musician or a writer to listen to your work. I've listened to computer databases, photocopiers, water running over dishes, and envelopes being stuffed. When I actively listen to my work—whatever the job—it suddenly has a compelling story. It always has something important to say.

GET INVOLVED WITH THE PROCESS

When you listen to your work, you are getting involved with the process moment by moment, day after day. You are like Helen, my sculptor neighbor, when she carves a Buddha from a large block of marble. Slowly, over the weeks, the outline of the body appears. Then come the hands in meditation mudra and the legs in full lotus. Finally Helen carves the face: half-open eyes, contemplative smile. I always love the smiles on Helen's Buddhas. Every time I see them, I not only see a smile of enlightenment, but I feel the inspiration in Helen's work as well.

As Helen carves, she listens to her work. She involves herself completely with the process. Some days she knows where she is going to carve and the texture of the lines she wants to make. Some days she isn't quite so sure, so she just polishes the stone, being patient as she considers the next step. Other days aren't about physically working; they are about living the rest of her life as fully and contentedly as she can and letting her work be.

Inspiration is like this. Listening. Getting involved with the process of what is in front of you, day after day. Watching for the elephants—and other possibilities—on the road. It's recognizing when it's time to live your life as completely as you can and let your work be. Inspiration is working with what you have right now, whether it's driving a truck, preparing a meal, typing a letter, or carving a sculpture. Sometimes you carve fine lines. Other times you just polish. Either way, you are chipping away, moment after moment, day after day. And after you chip enough, you begin to see something beautiful take form. Sometimes you even create a little Buddha in the process.

THE MYRIAD POSSIBILITIES

IN TODAY'S ever-changing job market, another way to get inspired is to entertain the myriad possibilities. Is she crazy? you may ask. Myriad possibilities, seriously, in this era of economic shifts and corporate restructuring? *No way, José.*

But yes, there really are a lot of options available to us, even as we wonder if they are becoming extinct. Even as we puzzle over the constant changes that confront us every day. In fact, economists and futurists report that the market isn't shrinking but is actually reshuffling, resulting in opportunities that didn't exist before. So there *are* a lot of possibilities. The keys here are to believe in their existence and be willing to seek them out.

You probably already suspect that this is going to be a practical job-hunting sort of chapter, and you are right. Because inspiration goes beyond imagination and attitude and internal worlds. It also involves getting down to the workaday basics of résumés and networking—applying inspiration to job hunting and professional advancement. It's about arming yourself with the necessary tools and using those tools to explore the possibilities. The thing about exploration is that in the beginning you may not be exactly certain where you're going. Or it may seem like you are going around and around—which you could be, because employment these days can feel a little like being on a hamster wheel. It can be frenetic. It can be a true test of reflexes and nerves. The good news is that, little by little, you build balance; you gain momentum. You begin to think on your feet. You even get past that dizzy feeling and find your sense of direction. You start to see your options—to feel inspired.

Whether you are searching for inspiration in a current situation or contemplating changing jobs, you might begin to tap in to these possibilities by considering

- The opportunities within your present job: its positive aspects, its potentials for advancement, and the fact that you are building your résumé with every project, every day.
- The many areas that you personally have to draw on: employment and educational background, professional and interpersonal skills, life experiences, the unique personality that you bring to a job, your attitude, and how you generally operate in the world.
- The hundreds of thousands of jobs in existence—literally hundreds for which you are probably more qualified than you think. And hundreds more for which you *can* be qualified if you upgrade your skills.

There is a lot to work with right here. Maybe more than you thought. The first step is to determine which possibilities you want to entertain. Then map out the next step and follow through.

RIGHT HERE, RIGHT NOW

Several years ago, a boss of mine went to a full-day seminar on marketing and statistics. On the podium next to the seminar facilitator was a cardboard box about the size of a toaster. Having been to his share of seminars, my boss knew that the box must have some kind of significance, but he didn't know what. He figured that at some poignant moment during the seminar, the purpose of that mystery box would be revealed.

As the day continued, however, the facilitator paid no attention to the box. She didn't place anything inside it or take anything from it. She didn't appear to notice the box at all.

Finally, about an hour before the seminar ended, my boss couldn't stand it any longer. He raised his hand and asked what was in the box. The facilitator smiled. Then she reached inside, pulled out a crisp hundred-dollar bill, and handed it to him. "That," she said, "is what you get for asking."

I always remember this story when I consider the many possibilities in employment. Because often the possibilities are right before your eyes, right here, right now. Like the half-written résumé inside your computer. Like the hidden hundred dollars inside the seminar box. It may even be as close as your current job.

Beginning with your present work, what *are* the positives—creative responsibilities, ongoing challenges, a strong personal belief in your company's service or product? What entices you to return day after day—inspiring coworkers, a pleasant environment, flexibility, personal recognition, satisfying financial compensation? Does the position hold deep meaning for you, or is it something more basic than that? What exactly is it that keeps you going back?

I talked to an office manager who swore that what kept her going to work was the fact that one of her colleagues made the best lemon charlotte to ever hit earth. Having once received a heavenly homemade cardamom birthday cake from a colleague, I could appreciate the sentiment. Still, I said, "But Arlene, is there anything you like about the *job*?" "Job?" she replied, her eyes glazed over. "Sure, it's fine. Oh, but that cake. . . ."

Cake aside, consider now your potentials for advancement. Are there potential challenges that could make your days more rewarding? Places where you might fill out your professional experience a little more? Maybe your company is announcing new developments or expanding into larger territories. Maybe there is sudden growth in established areas. Could it be that you have exactly what it takes to fill one of those slots?

The Myriad Possibilities   21

I know several professionals who jumped on the bandwagon by requesting upgrade transfers as new branches were added to their companies. Others have asked for additional responsibilities and subsequently upgraded their job titles. I also know a few enterprising employees who have created new jobs for themselves by pointing out a need for a position that didn't already exist—a new project leader, for example—writing a proposal outlining how that position would be effective for the organization and listing their own qualifications as the perfect candidate. Which goes to show that, like my boss and the mystery box, sometimes the possibilities are there for the asking.

Another facet of right here, right now is considering that every day you are building your résumé. Even if you don't have the job you want, every day you can be creating something to carry to a future situation. Take a look at your current responsibilities. Are they all on your résumé—every single one? Take a second look. Are you sure? Now think about anything you do that isn't in your job description. Is this listed on your résumé as well? If not, it should be, for every little thing you do on every job increases your future options.

Even if you aren't in the market for a new position, periodically updating your employment history is a good idea. It helps to review your skills, to assess where you need to grow, and to prepare you for new opportunities. Also, keeping regular track of your accomplishments can be a personal boost, as well as a reminder to your employer that a raise or promotion might be due.

Speaking of promotions, how flexible and versatile are you? These qualities are considered among the "universal skills" that every employer is looking for. Having them enhances the myriad possibilities. To employers, the most valuable employees are open to change, willing to learn new technology, and interested in taking on expanding roles. So the more you have to offer, the more employable you are.

Please don't misunderstand; I'm not talking Gumby here. I don't mean for anyone to turn green and bend into impossible contortions to meet your company's needs. But think of flexibility in the sense of being an expert in one area while spreading your professional wings. Consider it heightened security in the event of corporate restructuring. Or view it as simply the variety that is the spice of life.

Versatility may even be your road to advancement. I have a journalist colleague who has the abilities to work in several different areas of her newspaper and has been willing to move around as her paper needed to fill certain voids. Eventually her managing editor realized how valuable she was and promoted her to manager of her own department.

OUT THERE, SOMEWHERE

Okay, maybe those other people have managed to find opportunities in their current situations, but what if you can't see as much as one tiny oasis in your Sahara Desert of a job? What if you have given the current potentials every conceivable chance, have sifted through each grain of sand in your corporate wasteland, and there is nothing, nada, zilch? What if there is nary a scrawny cactus blooming and everywhere you look, it is drydrydry? It's baaaaaaad. I've had a few jobs like that myself.

So you think it's time to move on. It probably is. People change. Situations change. Our goals and philosophies grow beyond our present needs. A job that fit perfectly a year ago may now be way too small. So it's time to go shopping for a brand new professional outfit. Time to take a look around.

But what else is out there? you wonder. And how much? Remember: think myriad. Get your résumé in order, get serious about the search, and you will see.

TRANSCENDING YOUR RÉSUMÉ

A woman in one of my workshops said, "Life on paper is impossible. I'm thinking about transcending my résumé."

She meant this as a joke, but the more I thought about it, the more sense it made. Because in today's employment market, you have to work past your basic professional skills to get ahead. You have to give employers a glimpse of your potentials—not just your credentials—for them to get an idea of who you truly are.

One way to do this is by adding a short "additional skills" section to your résumé or curriculum vitae, along with your professional and educational backgrounds. Do you have computer literacy, interpersonal communication strengths, and the aforementioned universal skills? Include them in this section. Do you have the ability to work on a variety of teams, to adapt to advancing technology? Can you briefly illustrate how you have succeeded in these areas in the past? Write it all down, because studies show that businesses prefer to hire people with a wide range of skills. And maybe your particular range will be the lucky combination that nets the job.

A recent Purdue University survey of corporate recruiters reported that extracurriculars count, too. This means that volunteer work, hobbies, athletic activities, and other personal interests can make a difference in the hiring process. Employers do give these extras a serious look.

Keeping transcendence in mind, consider your personal experiences and interests. Think about those skills and talents that you don't necessarily need at work but have been applying elsewhere for a great while. Do any of them include marketable qualifications that might apply to your search? Might these interests enhance your viability as a job candidate?

Perhaps you developed organizational and delegation experience through directing your annual church fair for several years, as a friend of mine discovered when she went from being a stay-at-home mom to being a nonprofit organization's events planner. Perhaps your years of Zen meditation and study qualify you to teach meditation classes at your alma mater. One of my colleagues was an administrator before she entered the writing field. How did she make the switch? By listing on her résumé the series of articles she had published in parenting magazines, she found a writing position in the public schools.

One of my favorite stories in this category involves a friend who turned a longtime personal photography interest into a full-time career. After being let go from his public relations position at a publishing house, he managed to support himself and his family by doing freelance marketing assignments. Meanwhile, he refined his photographic talents, built up his portfolio, and displayed his work in several shows. Three years later, it all paid off. When a nearby university department had an opening for a staff photographer, he was in the right place at the right time to fill the bill.

In considering personal interest areas, dig deep. Look hard. You may uncover some long-forgotten skills. Be creative in directing those skills, add a lot of enthusiasm and an equal amount of perseverance, and you may find yourself transcending your résumé into the perfect job.

VALUES

These days there is a lot of talk about values as they relate to jobs. Values in terms of aligning your personal philosophy with your livelihood. Values as applied to making a significant contribution to society within the context of your work. Just how do values fit into this idea of transcendence? How do they fit into the myriad possibilities?

This reminds me of Dar, a frustrated electrical engineer who underwent career counseling to determine a new career path. The first question his counselor posed had to do with values. Were there some industries that were aligned with Dar's personal philosophy and others that he couldn't bring himself to pursue? Did he view a job solely as a means of income, or did he believe it should be an avenue for helping others? What about the issue of significant contribution: would any job connected with his skills and interests do, or did he want a situation with deep, deep meaning?

For the first time in his life, Dar began to seriously ponder his answers to these questions. No, he didn't want to work in a nuclear weapons plant. Of course, he wasn't comfortable with a business that exploited child labor in third world countries. Yes, he would like to be associated with a company that contributed significantly to the well-being of humanity and the environment. And certainly he felt it important to take social responsibility in his life and in his work.

Still, Dar wondered, just how far do you take these ideas? Just how far do you go before you begin to limit your possibilities and those of your family? For example, was it necessary to find a job that developed products that were good for the environment or advocated children's rights? Or, given the proper attitude, could he make a significant contribution within just about any job? Did he need to join the Peace Corps to help others—or could he be a positive force in any workplace by giving his all, by being respectful and kind, and by being completely present with each person he encountered? What *about* "meaningful" work—did true meaning come from the job itself, or did it start within?

At this writing, Dar is still pondering these questions. Within their context, he continues to search for a new career. At the same time, he has made a few changes in his life by going part time with his job, spending more hours on Zen practice, and considering his values at a basic level. This includes being a positive force in his current workplace by listening fully and going one step beyond merely doing his fair share, and increasing his awareness of humanity and the environment by paying more attention to the world around him. Later, he will see about expanding on these values. But, for now, he is concentrating on the concepts of "do no harm" and "leave only a positive trace."

THE WAITING GAME

It wouldn't be fair to have a chapter on possibilities and not talk about the fact that sometimes you have to wait. Yes, I hear the groans . . . but employment, like anything else in life, is a matter of timing. That time could be today. It could be three months or a year from now. Either way, time is on its own schedule, meaning you sometimes have to play the waiting game.

During waiting periods, I try to remind myself that patience is a virtue. Unfortunately, it's also one of life's nasty little nightmares—something that most of us would rather avoid. The one good thing about patience is that it buys time. Time to build skills and clarity. Time to moderate, to get organized, to make contacts. Time to do a little extra meditation prior to a busier time.

Why do some people find new jobs right away and others have a very long wait? I don't know. I'll go merrily along with work falling into my lap from every direction, then suddenly every possibility falls between the cracks. Is it something I said? Ooooooh. Something I did? Ahhhh. Does my résumé have bad breath, even though I doused it with mouthwash before sending it off? At this point, I notice that I'm getting a little carried away with the process, so I generally take a step back. And I ask myself, Should I reconsider my expectations? Alter my approach? Or do I need to stop taking it personally and face the fact that the situation may be simply the luck of the draw?

Sometimes a short-term setback may set the scene for long-term advancement, as in the case of Jill, who had a master's degree in educational psychology but couldn't find a job in her field. Desperate for work, she finally took an administrative position with a high-tech corporation through a temporary staffing service while she played the waiting game. By doing an excellent job, showing her psychology skills, and, most importantly, networking with the right people, one year later she was able to maneuver herself into a branch of her company called "human factors"—the department that applies psychology to advancing technology.

I know another person who played a lot of solitary chess as he strategized a major career move for seven years. He was so quiet, so intense, that his wife said he was planning a revolution. It turned out he was. Finally, he made a career change that happily turned their lives upside down. Now, as an officer in the State Department, he rarely plays much chess at all. He is too busy working around the world.

———————

Yes, the myriad possibilities are out there. Especially when you know how much you have to offer and what you're looking for. The possibilities may be in your very own workplace, or you may find yourself on a roundabout route as you play the waiting game. Either way, think about what you have to gain in the process and how wonderful it will feel when you maneuver yourself into the job of your choice.

Getting In

CREATIVE NETWORKING

WE HEAR a lot about how networking is the most important way to find a job, and this can't be emphasized enough, because people of all kinds are at the center of the myriad possibilities. Yes, I've heard the rumor that networking has a bad reputation these days, and yes, I know it's hard as heck, but since personal contacts are the most direct route to the greatest variety of jobs and since only 20 percent of all openings are actually advertised in the newspaper, networking is still the best avenue to gainful employment. The key is to network thoughtfully and creatively. And—of course—the larger the network, the better.

Think your network is small? At first I thought mine was, too. Once I started jotting down a few names, however, I was amazed at how they began to multiply. After you recall previous employers, colleagues, clients, family members, neighbors, friends, and friends of friends, you will undoubtedly be reminded of others in your midst who might be able to open a few doors—members of your church or Zen center, fellow volunteers at the community food co-op, black belts (and brown belts and yellow belts and polka-dotted belts) from your aikido class, parents of your children's friends, and that nice Ezekiel Rumpletoff from your monthly book group whose Aunt Myrtle just happens to be vice president at Company X. Add to this the potential of creating new contacts through avenues like seminars, job clubs, the Internet, and, well, just serendipity, and I bet you will find that your network is larger—and more creative—than you thought.

The British philosopher Francis Bacon said that a wise person makes more opportunities than he finds. Applied to the job search, I like to interpret this advice as "Make your life your network." This means that everything you do and everywhere you go has network possibilities, both for now and for the future. Yes, yes, yes, everyone you meet is a potential job contact. I don't suggest this in the sense of taking unfair advantage of associates and colleagues or pushing products you are selling on unsuspecting friends. I only mean that when you have an awareness of who is in your midst, you will be more open to possible contacts.

A friend of mine found her teaching position through an ex-colleague whose current boss lived next door to the principal of a local elementary school. Another friend moved into her biotech job through an internship where, as she said, she "distributed résumés to everyone walking slowly enough to hand one to." And one time, after a talk I gave on alternative workstyles at a city-sponsored job club, a woman followed me into the hallway—not to discuss my topic, but to ask how she could get her book published. After admiring her resourcefulness, I was happy to share a few ideas.

When your life is your network, you never know what you will find.

I have been offered jobs by happenstance at parties, in bookstores, on airplanes, in coffeehouses, and while hiking in the White Mountains of New Hampshire—all through casual conversation. One time I was asked to write a grant for a landscaper I met in the rosebush section of a gardening center, and I even found a freelance opportunity while waiting in a checkout line at Woolworth's in Boston. The line was long that day, and during the wait I chatted with the gentleman behind me—a poet who had written over a thousand poems but hadn't marketed them because he was afraid of rejection.

By the time we got to the cashier, I had an appointment with him to discuss taking on the assignment of being his poetry agent, a task that involved submitting his poems to literary magazines and anthologies and informing him only of the acceptances. After interviewing him further—he was independently wealthy, a philanthropist who gave most of his time to charities when he wasn't writing poetry—and reading all one thousand poems, most of which I liked, we agreed to a flat rate for my services, plus a commission on each accepted piece. I subsequently spent much of the following year placing several of his poems in publications across the country, after which he returned to the Bahamas, where he was going to manage his family estate, and I moved on to other projects.

In general, I've discovered that I'm most successful when I view job-hunting periods as very social times of my life. Because socializing is the difference between plain old-fashioned ho-hum networking and creative connections. Because a little spontaneous conversation may be the fine line between buying a cheap pair of scissors at Woolworth's and netting an interesting freelance assignment. Besides, conversing keeps you socially limber, which is good practice for the interviews that will be happening very soon. And it has you out there exercising, maybe even *aerobicizing*, your options.

So socialize. Talk to people at work, at community gatherings, in line at the grocery store, at the recreation center, on commuter trains, anywhere (dark alleys excepted) there seems to be an opening to communicate. You never know when someone will say something that will give you a great idea, a contact—or even a job.

INFORMATION GATHERING, TELEPATHY, AND OTHER NETWORKING SOURCES

Information gathering is an excellent avenue for creative networking if you are willing to read beyond the lines. Newspapers, radio, magazines, and television can all provide valuable updates on employment trends and organizational developments. They are loaded with job-hunting connections in the form of articles, advertisements, lists, and short features. Also, you may be surprised to discover that seemingly mundane sources such as the Yellow Pages, community directories, and business newsletters offer listings that often have clues about the top business opportunities in your field.

One of my colleagues found her marketing position at a nonprofit organization through a listing in her city's small business tabloid. She promptly gave the business a call and discovered that it was looking for a new marketing coordinator; she subsequently made the director a pitch he couldn't refuse. Similarly, I once created my own creative-director position through a newspaper article and a little telepathy. Okay, maybe it wasn't exactly telepathy, but some sort of synchronicity was obviously at work, because at the time I was considering a new job I saw a newspaper story about a local publishing company. On a whim, I contacted the publisher who, as it turned out, was considering expanding his staff. Coincidentally, one of the new positions required my specific combination of writing and design skills, a situation some of my friends would describe as the universe looking out for me and I would refer to as a little well-organized telepathy. Anyway, after several follow-up meetings, during which we exchanged work philosophies and astrological signs (although neither of us knew much about astrology at the time), we established a strong rapport that continued throughout the three years I managed his university-oriented publications.

THE INTERNET

Internet job connections are particularly plentiful in a wide range of areas. According to the *Wall Street Journal*, there are *more than half a million job postings on any given day* on the top fifteen online job banks—including America's Job Bank, an Internet service of the U.S. Department of Labor. Employees who use the Net, tell success stories of finding work more quickly after being laid off, having easier out-of-state job access, and enjoying the benefits of more expeditious responses. Job seekers can also take advantage of online career centers, which offer career guidance, résumé-writing tips, and more. This network for job hunting is growing. So if you aren't online, it may be time to get hooked up. If you don't have a computer at home, check out academic and business career centers and public libraries, many of which offer job-line access. I know several professionals who have found a wealth of work via this avenue, including jobs abroad and work-at-home opportunities.

HUMAN-SIZED COMPANIES

While you are leafing through your local newspaper and business guides, consider what Duane Elgin, author of *Voluntary Simplicity*, calls "human-sized companies": organizations with two hundred or fewer employees. As opposed to the Abominable Snowman–like demeanors of many megacorporations, these companies are generally easier to approach, offer unexpected growth potential, and are often more willing to give you a chance if you are changing careers. They are frequently more open to individual creativity as well as providing opportunities to develop your skills in a variety of areas of the business. This also gives you a few different directions in which to advance.

At the same time, look at companies that operate globally. According to futurists, businesses that focus on areas beyond their own geographical region are more stable because they have a larger vision and are able to tap into an international economy. There are a number of small firms that keep a low profile but maintain quite successful worldwide connections. Don't underestimate the power of these companies. Many of them do an annual multimillion-dollar business and have clients from some of the largest organizations all over the world. It's well worth finding out what this market requires and where you might fit in.

TEMPORARY STAFFING ASSIGNMENTS

Temporary assignments can be a great source of networking opportunities. Since contract work exists in just about every field, the short-term job route is a smart way to get a foot in the door of not just one but several businesses. Temporary staffing has especially become popular in the form of temp-to-hire jobs, because employers prefer to hire people they know, both personally and professionally. This is a good system for job hunters, too, as it affords them opportunities to assess employers before entertaining an offer.

Have a company in mind that you would like to check out? Try calling its human resources department and asking if they directly hire contractors in your field. If so, find out what you need to do to begin the application process. In the event that the company only contracts through a staffing service, ask which agencies they use. Then sign up with those agencies and request to be sent to that business as appropriate assignments come up. I have several colleagues who have done this—with the desired results. Some eventually got on full-time with their prospective firm. A few found the particular company not to be what they were looking for at all, so they went on to connect with businesses that were more compatible with their goals. Others, including my accountant friend Valerie, made valuable contacts through temporary assignments that netted them numerous projects for years to come.

Many people discover that the temporary staffing network takes them in directions they never would have imagined. This happened with a colleague who accepted a short-term writing assignment and ended up managing a company's conference-planning group. Another acquaintance signed on with a corporation as a temporary office assistant and advanced to full-time corporate travel agent. Which goes to show that this network is not only full of creative possibilities but has the potential for hidden surprises as well.

––––––––––––

Admittedly, networking can at times be akin to an aerobic workout of the nerves—not to mention a true test of the soul—but today's employment market demands perseverance. You may be the most talented, intelligent, experienced, and spiritual person on earth, but employers won't know that unless you tell them. So get on the phone. Knock on doors. Write letters. Load up your résumé gun, stand atop the tallest skyscraper you know, and shoot your résumés into the air. Send up rockets. Hire a skywriter to write your outstanding qualifications in purple smoke outside the picture window of your favorite potential employers if that's what it takes. Well, maybe you won't need to go quite *that* far, but you will want to take a deep breath, take your vitamins, go to your yoga class, check in with a good friend for moral support—and follow up again and again.

Networking should be kept within reason, of course. I heard about a young writer who was so eager for work that she followed a well-known magazine editor into the rest room at a conference and slid her publication clippings to the editor beneath the stall. Needless to say, she didn't get the job—and she probably burned a bridge in the process. True, a bridge she never quite had to begin with, but it could have reached its potential if she had only given it the proper chance.

As the saying goes, "Moderation in everything, including moderation." Even in networking. Because, like anything else in life, a network functions best when treated with propriety and respect. When approached with dignity and confidence, but not overconfidence. You want to get your name on the list, but, as an HR director I know says, "There is a good list and a bad list. You want to get on the right one."

Of course, there will be times when you don't get on the list at all. Which is fine, because when you network creatively you know that not every contact is going to pan out. So you learn to accept "no" without taking it personally and to say, "I understand" with grace. Maybe the polka-dotted belt from your aikido class doesn't have the awesome contacts you thought. Maybe Ezekiel Rumpletoff's Aunt Myrtle is infinitely impressed with your qualifications, but she doesn't have any openings right now. She might keep you in her file or pass your name along to another CEO with whom she power lunches once a week. Then again, nothing may come of it at all, for which you will later thank her when her "rejection" makes room for a better opportunity down the road.

In the event of no response whatsoever, which everyone tells me is a major trend these days, remember that employers get bzillions of pieces of paper and even more telephone calls, of which yours is only one. Yes, it's rude of someone not to respond in some form, even if it is only a form letter. Especially when you have outstanding qualifications, have written *the* cover letter of the century, and have communicated every way to get in touch with you, from your E-mail address to the number of your pager, which you even keep with you by the bath. But heck, in your next life when you are that person's mother, you can teach her a manner or two. Meanwhile, in this life, take another deep breath, reload your résumé gun, and shift your focus to another employer.

Then persevere, persevere, persevere. In the wise words of the *I Ching*, "Calm and correct persistence brings good fortune." And it does. It truly does. Take it from *moi*, the most persistent person to ever hit earth. With perseverance, you are guaranteed to convince a few potential employers (and probably more) that you are a valuable job candidate—*and* the right person for the job.

PREDICTING THE PAST

IF YOU want to open up to the future, to give yourself more possibilities in terms of work, sometimes it's helpful to predict the past. To do what Rob Brezsny, a gutsy astrologer whose column I sometimes read, calls a "postdiction." Understanding where you are now—and where you might strive to be—through taking a look at where you've been. By predicting your past.

Now, as a rule, I'm not crazy about analyzing my childhood. Nor, for that matter, am I hot on mucking around in my past thousand lives (during many of which, I'm convinced, I was a dimorphic jumping spider in a Zen monastery in Japan). Generally, I prefer to concentrate on the here and now. But when I want to make sense of why I am a writer instead of a banker, or why I chose a variety of jobs over one lifetime position in the corporate sector (if such an animal still exists), it helps to take a mental trip inward. To get together with friends over a mocha latté and spy on the past.

Why bother? you may ask. What does the past have to do with now? What's the point in looking back when you can only change what is happening today?

Because when you postdict, you can find threads to the reasons you chose a particular path—or left another behind. And when you're more aware of these threads, you can give yourself more options to weave them differently the next time they come around.

Because it can be immensely clarifying to relocate the old threads that kept you on the straight and narrow, and the ones that suggested, à la baseball legend Yogi Berra, "When you come to a fork in the road, take it."

Because in traveling back to that fork, you may begin to recognize the voices that supported you in your efforts, as opposed to the ones that still haunt you in your darkest hour. Maybe you know those voices. They are the ones that plunk down heavily on the side of the bed in the middle of the night and mess up your dreams with raggedy little messages like, "I *told* you to be a stockbroker, Angeline. Now, look at you, a starving artist, tsk, tsk tsk. Isn't it time to get a respectable job?"

In taking a backward look around, you can view these messages right up close and see how they influence you in the choices you make today. You can appreciate an artist who visited your school in seventh grade and understand how his personal attention encouraged you to pursue your dreams. You can realize how a special teacher gave you a little push in your music career by telling you how much she loved your musical voice. You can see what a difference it made in your life to be taken under a writer neighbor's wing at the tender age of fifteen. The beauty of postdiction is that the more you work with it, the more voices resound from your past. As you postdict, you can listen a little more for the ones you want to hear.

In predicting the past, you can also work a little more with the negative voices that might be interfering with your work and your life. You can see how, even though you went ahead to become an artist against your family's wishes, deep down you feel guilty because you didn't follow in your father's stockbroker footsteps. You can see how, even though you forged your own path, deep down you still feel shame because you didn't do what you were "supposed to do." And because of that guilt and shame, you aren't quite as successful in your work as you know you could be. Those negative voices have been gnawing at you, getting in the way, holding you back.

A psychotherapist friend of mine helps his clients to overcome negative voices by invoking the power of his "cotherapist,"

Mrs. Sabotini. He says, "When I was a child, there was an old Italian woman in my neighborhood. Practically raised me and a few others. She told me one day, 'You must betray me and go your own way. Don't listen to me anymore. Find your own voice now. And go.' " Through postdiction, you can activate your own Mrs. Sabotini, tell those voices you won't listen to them anymore. You can very kindly inform them that you appreciate their concern, but you've made your choices, thank you very much. From now on you intend to work to your fullest potential, and in order to do that you can only welcome voices that give you strength. Finally, you can tell them, sternly if necessary, please, with organic turbinado sugar on top, please just go away.

If you think about it, a few of our attitudes about work were probably formed not long after we were born. Picture this. Your parents are at the dinner table, discussing their days. Your mother, a university professor, is talking excitedly about her freshman math class. Your father, an accountant, is frustrated that his boss doesn't understand the first thing about his complex numbers. You, in your high chair, finger painting lovely pictures with your strained carrots and peas, are the captive audience. What else are you going to do—read the annotated *War and Peace*? Where else are you going to go—on a Caribbean cruise?

I don't think so. No, you have no choice but to do a little accidental eavesdropping, and it may not be the actual words that strike you, but the *tone*—a tone of excitement or boredom or annoyance or whatever—that endures at the table for years to come. A tone that may not have made much of an impression at that formative age, but one that weasels into your delicate senses, weaves its way through your thought processes, and eventually gives you your first attitudes, maybe even lifelong attitudes, about employment. There is a lot of old influence going on there.

Look at your family. Your family's family. Look at your neighbors, your parents' friends, your friends' parents. Recall your teachers, your spiritual leaders, a gypsy tarot reader you met on vacation in Virginia Beach the summer you were ten. Remember the Russian artist upstairs who posed nude for university drawing classes—you couldn't believe this was actually somebody's job.

Set up the VCR inside your head and run a few tapes of these old stories in the back of your head. Reclaim a few of the old movies that you may have forgotten. Consider the story of your great-grandmother who moved to Boston alone in the mid-1800s and opened a hat shop, a daring venture for a woman in those days. Recall your great-uncle who taught at Cornell University—not anything academic like English or history, but the fine art of making cheese. Remember the cousin who became a hospice worker after accidentally backing over her father with his own Model T in his icy driveway, and your twin aunts who were always doing everyone's astrological charts. And what about your grandfather who had about a million careers—the grandfather who taught you about driving and working and who always said, "There are many ways to make a living. Do them all if you want, but do it with self-respect."

Once you have taken a look at the videotapes, take a look at your reactions. The ones you had then and the ones you have now. Did these stories encourage you toward what you really wanted to do in work, or did they start you on the trail of somebody else's goals? Did they point you toward a traditional career, or were they factors to persuade you to take a more unusual route? Did you make those choices independently, or based on what someone else thought you should do?

In my case, I embraced a few of the nontraditional values despite the wishes of my parents, who wanted me to do something safe like be a librarian or teach second grade. In fact, I realize now, I followed my distant relatives quite closely. I took on the attitudes of the grandmother who was independent of the status quo, even moving alone to Boston (and a few other places). Like my great-uncle, I have taught classes that weren't in the usual academic vein. Even as we speak, I find myself walking in the footprints of my grandfather with the million careers, as I see more and more possibilities in livelihood. Goodness, I didn't realize until I wrote this paragraph how much I followed those messages, how much they pulled me along. Which is what I mean by postdiction. It opens you up. It clears the path. It is like taking a photograph of yourself and watching it develop. It helps you get to where you want to go.

Fortunately, I like where I'm going. Most of the time, that is. But there are moments, such as when I'm doing corporate project work or when an editor wants to change my copy too much, that I find myself getting stuck. These are the times when a spontaneous postdiction tells me I'm coloring too much outside the lines, that my free spirit is being a little too creative for its own good. A few extra guidelines can be beneficial to the overall process once in a while, my postdiction points out. This is when I need to pay attention. To remind myself that there are other voices than the ones I originally followed—voices with important things to say.

Predicting the past may open a new door for you as it did with Erin, who once ran her own collection agency with two other partners. Although the business was very successful, when sheer misery finally forced her to sell her share, she couldn't decide what direction to take next. As she brainstormed about her past, Erin grasped a long-forgotten thread—the fact that she had always wanted to be a nurse, but her mother wanted her to be a doctor. To keep the peace, she did neither and went to business school instead. After working through this postdiction, she realized that her mother no longer influenced her career path. She was free to do whatever she wished, which eventually turned out to be nursing school.

Postdiction also provided a few insights for Wes, a marketing manager who for the longest time couldn't understand why he didn't get the preferred results from his staff. He was a good manager, he was fair, he had an open-door policy. What was the problem? he wanted to know. In looking back, he saw his father, a four-star general, giving strict orders around the house. As Wes appreciated out loud his father's strong leadership role, both then and now, he saw that he himself had been inadvertently imitating the military method of management—a style appropriate for the army, but not for his marketing group.

After the postdiction, Wes began to work toward a different approach, with a positive outcome for both himself and his staff. Now, when he hears himself speaking in the general's voice, he gives himself a salute and exerts more effort toward leaving it in the past.

I'm not suggesting that we get too caught up in this idea of postdiction. Nor am I talking deep, dark analysis—unless you have issues a therapist might help to resolve. And I'm surely not recommending that we predict our colleagues' pasts—oh no, no, no. But try a little backward time traveling sometime when there is nothing pressing over the lunch hour or when your computer just crashed and you can't do a thing until it comes back on. Try it during one of those oh-so-yawnish staff meetings when you are wondering how the heck you got to this particular workplace on Mars. On one of these occasions, take a peek at where you're going, based on where you've been.

Just the other day my horoscope by Rob said, "Your dream job, which may have been a million miles away as late as yesterday, may suddenly be no farther than a stone's throw." When I read that, I couldn't help smiling. Could this be the result of my latest postdiction? Could I have brought myself closer to that dream job by predicting the past? I guess it's a definite possibility.

I highly recommend postdiction. It can be illuminating and rejuvenating. It can be seriously liberating. It can even make you strong.

CLIMBING MOUNTAINS—
AND JOBS

AFTER GRADUATING from college, I moved two thousand miles across the country to a town I'd never seen, with the intent of landing my first full-time job and thus, as I saw it, marking my passage into adulthood. I chose this particular town because it was fresh territory, a distant frontier, and because it leaned up against the Rocky Mountains—which I viewed as appropriately symbolic of my ascent into the workaday world. In fact, I sent out silly announcement poems before my departure:

> *Graduation accomplished*
> *I will now scale mountains*
> *and soar to new heights*
> *Caw, caw.*

Yes, I was primed for success, and within a week of arrival I netted a production/design position at the daily newspaper—a victory I gained over ninety other applicants because I was the only one to make a follow-up call. So I had my first real job, maybe even the Great American Job. I was off to meet new challenges, and I have to admit that I felt pretty important. My head was aswirl with visions of grand accomplishments and enough money to do whatever I liked. I was about to scale mountains. And soar to new heights.

The working world being what it is, full of surprises and challenges and all species of colleagues, within six months I was ready to get off the mountain. Not that I wanted to climb down forever—just for a week or so. After all, the air was a little thinner up there than I'd expected. I needed time to acclimate. I needed to get some objectivity in the form of something I had so far only heard rumors about: a paid vacation.

Unfortunately, this didn't seem to be what the employment gods had in mind. Because when I took this request to my supervisor, he didn't seem to understand. Didn't I like the job? he asked. Sure, I said. How about my coworkers—did I enjoy working with them? They were fine, I assured him. Then what was the problem? he wanted to know. No problem, I said, I just need a serious break.

My supervisor sighed. He shook his head. Hadn't I read the employee handbook? he asked. Weeell, I replied, not *exactly*. Specifically, page 66? he wanted to know. I had to admit I hadn't looked at the handbook at all. My supervisor shook his head again. Finally, very kindly, he explained the reality of the situation: I wasn't eligible for vacation for another six months.

At first I felt a jolt, as if someone had just applied electroshock therapy full-force to my head. Next I felt myself going numb. Then sheer panic overtook me, claustrophobia clutching at my throat. Uh-oh, I gulped. I think I've made a terrible mistake. After running from his office, reading the handbook, and calculating that I had forty-three and a half years of employment before I would be eligible for retirement, the next day I did what I thought was only reasonable under the circumstances: I called in sick. And then I flew to California for a week to walk the beach and judge my plight.

The verdict? Guilty as charged. I realized there was no way I was going to make it through those forty-three years if I didn't take a better look at what I was getting into. If I continued to view employment as a life sentence and my workplace as a jail. Clearly,

I would have to find a different way to scale the mountain, or I was never going to get to the top.

LEARNING THE ROPES

Every mountain looks the same at its base: enormous. For some this is intimidating, for others a challenge. I am somewhere in between. With my first encounter, I think, Ohmygod, where do I start? Then I remember the challenge aspect, the curiosity of what I will find there, and I am ready to go.

When I encountered that mountain of my first job, I saw myself on an expedition. I couldn't wait to get on my rubbery shoes and start the climb. Yes, I know it seems kind of crazy to be that eager to work, but I really was. I wanted to learn what this new world of employment was all about. That is, until I hit my first real obstacle; then I wanted to take a different route.

What I didn't know about mountains and jobs is that

- You have to be prepared.
- You have to learn the ropes.
- Everyone has a different style.
- You have to keep working at it.
- Sometimes you have to improvise.
- The weather isn't always going to be what you expect.

I also didn't know that in order to succeed and do it with spirit, I had to understand that I probably wouldn't be getting my wings right away. It was going to take much more than enthusiasm to do the job. Plain and simple, I would have to hunker down, get completely involved, and take the process step by step.

Being prepared involves being in shape, mentally and physically. This means having the right tools to do the work and arming yourself with as much information as possible in advance so you have a sense of what you're getting into. You wouldn't attempt to climb a mountain without adequate equipment, proper maps, and some knowledge of the expertise this mountain requires. You want to be cautioned about sudden, fierce animals, about the probable challenges on this particular route.

The same applies to a job, whether it's your first foray into the working world or your hundredth freelance assignment. You want to go into a position with an understanding of your job description, the hours, the rules, the rest stops, the company's expectations, and the people you will encounter. As I learned the hard way on my first job, you want a few concrete ideas about what to expect.

Learning the ropes entails learning to maneuver yourself upward and forward, watching carefully to get a feel for when it's time to hold on tight, when you should allow some slack, and when you need to work closely with the people on your team. In the case of climbing mountains, this sometimes means rappelling *backwards* down the rocks, with someone else in charge of the rope—yikes!—something I never did get used to. In other words, climbing involves teamwork and a great deal of trust.

Work is like this, too. You learn who is in charge of the ropes, how to work with them, the people you can count on, and those you definitely don't want on the other end of your rope. A corporate lawyer friend of mine who is on his third job told me that although he felt confident in his work he found times when he needed to ask his senior partner for help. This came as a surprise to him because he thought he knew everything necessary to do his job. He thought he already knew the ropes. Instead, he discovered that the experience of his colleague was invaluable, plus she offered insights that helped to advance him in his work.

Everyone has a different style means that there are many ways to climb and work. Some mountaineers use ropes, others climb freestyle. Some have their sights set on Mount Everest. Others are content to run up the smaller rocks—a technique called bouldering.

The same is true with employment. When I began climbing my mountain, who said I had forty-three years to go until retirement? Who said one-job-for-life was my style? Yes, some people love their work so much that they stay with one situation until they retire, while others change jobs every year or so. Still others leave a longtime situation at the age of fifty and start their own businesses or begin new careers. Many writers, artists, and musicians keep their passions alive until the day they die. Nuns and monks never retire, they just slow down. There are so many options, so many ways to get to the top. Everyone has to find his or her personal style.

Working at it takes into consideration that the situation isn't likely to run itself; you have to create the momentum to make it happen. The mountain isn't going to extend a hand, but it does have natural footholds for support if you seek them out. Similarly, a job can't be programmed to finish the tedious tasks while you hang out at the new espresso bar down the street, as I would sometimes like to do. Rather, every task deserves mindful attention, and in return you gain expertise. Once you get into the rhythm of it, this process can take you a long way toward overcoming obstacles as well as advance you to new levels—again and again and again.

Improvising is about working with whatever circumstances come up. It's about being flexible enough to work around a boulder on the path, a change in a deadline, a moody manager who makes last-minute decisions. Maybe this foothold or format will work; maybe that one is better. Improvising is being open to new possibilities along the way. For example, I once had a boss who said, "You do it and I'll tell you what's wrong" when he gave me a publication to design. If I asked for guidelines, he simply shrugged and replied that he would know what he liked when he saw it. Not knowing what else to do, I went to work—and came up frustrated time after time. Finally, I improvised by rounding up a stack of magazines and asking him what he liked and disliked about each one. As he pointed out his preferences, I thought, Okay, now we're cooking. And I was able to be a success in my work.

The weather isn't always going to be what you expect. In fact, it will probably change the minute your back is turned. You may feel sunny in the morning, only to have a grouchy colleague rain on your parade later in the day. Maybe your climb begins with blue sky and later there's an unpredictable thunderstorm. Once when my cousin John Patrick had climbed nearly to the top of a mysterious mountain called Big Gnarly, the sky suddenly grew dark. Of course, he thought it was cloud cover, but when he looked up, he sighted several hundred turkey vultures circling overhead. What did he do? Well, after a moment of apprehension, he just kept climbing. After all, he quickly reasoned, this was the most challenging mountain he had ever ascended, he wasn't dead meat, and he was almost there. And what were a few hundred vultures besides another interesting part of the trip? After they flew on and he reached the top, he said, "Man, you wouldn't have believed the view."

This is the way it is with mountains and jobs. There are always a few surprises, and if you keep this in mind you will be more prepared. Sometimes there is a torrential downpour. Sometimes the sky is full of vultures. Either way, if you're paying attention, it probably won't be boring. And after the storm—or the vulture invasion—is over, there may be one heck of a view.

TAKING IN THE LARGER VIEW

In his anthology *A Policy of Kindness*, the Dalai Lama wrote:

> In jobs, such as working for a company, or as a factory worker, even though you may not be directly helping others, indirectly you are serving society. Even though you are doing it for the sake of your salary, indirectly it does help people and you should do it with good motivation, trying to think, "my work is meant to help people."

At the point of my escape to California, although I was studying at a Buddhist meditation center, I didn't quite see employment as something beyond myself, as serving society or helping people. That is, I didn't see the larger view. Because I was relatively new to the workforce, I saw a job as merely a job—a place to perform X number of tasks in exchange for X amount of money. I thought that by giving Y amount of effort, I would receive exactly Y number of perks in return, all in accordance with my personal expectations.

I had part of this right. Although I understood that employment is about give and take, I wasn't clear about the giving part. I did know that I needed to give my all, but I didn't think of myself as part of a larger community, working with others toward a common goal. I didn't consider how my responsibilities at the newspaper contributed to the whole of the company, let alone how they might be related to the greater good of society. Mainly I wondered, What's in it for *me*?

As it turned out, there was quite a lot of personal gain. I remained at the newspaper for another year, during which I realized more personal benefit than I had expected. A creative job that I was learning from. A satisfactory wage. Pleasant colleagues who were serious about both work and fun. Plus a solid work base that I later used to springboard into more advanced publication positions. At the same time, I began to see the bigger picture. I began to understand how my role at the newspaper fit into the greater community. In my individual way, I was helping to give others a larger view with my small part in creating awareness about what was happening around the globe.

I never did master the fine art of technical climbing, although I was up on the ropes a few dizzying times before deciding that an alternative route was more my style. However, I did realize how alive I felt when I gave my full attention to the climb, no matter the method I used to ascend. Not only that, but I realized I was soaring to new awareness of both mountains and jobs. Which, now that I think about it, is the ultimate goal.

Another Perspective
on Freedom

Little did I know that, a few years later, the employment gods would send me to jail. Yes, at the base of the same mountain, only a few miles from the newspaper of my first job, I found a different sort of publication position—one that involved murderers, rapists, child molesters, car thieves, house burglars, drug dealers, and other criminals on a daily basis. That is, I spent one year doing intake interviews, and writing up their results, inside a Colorado county jail.

Imagine a job where, hour after hour, day after day, your assignment is to ask people the most personal questions about their lives. Imagine looking complete strangers in the eye (strangers who are inmates) and inquiring in detail about their childhoods, parents, employment histories, and intimate relationships. Consider sitting two feet from a murderer and asking him details about his sex life as if it were business as usual.

Next imagine analyzing the pattern of responses, adding in your personal impressions, and writing up a formal report to indicate an appropriate rehabilitation program for each inmate's needs—if indeed rehabilitation is possible. This was what my work was like that year.

The office where I conducted the interviews was a very small room deep inside the jail. It contained only a table, two chairs, and a surveillance camera. To get there I had to traverse a labyrinth of corridors connected by heavy locked doors. The doors were unlocked by armed guards in bulletproof control rooms, then locked behind me again. I can still hear the click of those locks following me down the hallways as I made my way to work each day and repeated the process on the way back out. I can still see the surveillance cameras watching me, recording my every move.

Often, as I left, an inmate would say, "I wish I could walk out the door." (Ironically, a phrase I've heard frequently from full-time employees when I've finished a contract job.) In truth, I wished many of them could leave, too. Some had shared their poetry, their watercolors, their deepest dreams with me. I had meditated and said mantras with a few. I saw that although they had committed crimes, at their hearts they were still human beings the same as me. And they wanted what everybody wants: to live with their families and be part of the world. They wanted one more chance to live free.

As it turned out, several of the inmates did have the opportunity to leave. Some became eligible for work release programs that involved day jobs outside the jail. Some were paroled, returned to their families, and were able to find well-paying jobs. But a large number of them were transferred to federal prisons. For years— maybe even for the rest of their lives—they would hear the eerie echo of the locks and be under the watchful eye of the cameras. They would have to live with these constant reminders that freedom for them was a thing of the past.

WHAT DOES FREEDOM REALLY MEAN?

You can imagine the reactions I had at my next job—a copy-writing position with a large communications company—as I waited at my desk on the first day for a guard to escort me through the halls. Okay, maybe my transition from the jail to the corporate sector wasn't *that* extreme. But it did take me a while to grasp the reality of the situation: I could leave on my own at any time.

When it finally hit me, I had a strong urge to camp on the intercom and make a few inspiring announcements:

"Guess what? We can go to the bathroom without asking permission!"

"Psssssst . . . we can scratch our noses without being under surveillance."

And, "Hallelujah, no automatic locks! We can leave the building whenever we like!"

I managed to restrain myself, knowing that my new colleagues would certainly call the white coats in three seconds flat. But I came oh-so-close on numerous occasions. Itchingly close. Screamingly close. Because in my mind important headline news was breaking: *We are volunteers in the workplace! As employees, we are absolutely amazingly incredibly utterly FREE.*

Awestruck by this discovery, I examined my career thus far. My production/design job at the newspaper, where I felt like I was in jail and had a desperate need to escape. My intake interview position, where my workplace literally was a jail. And my current copy-writing situation, where I was practically swinging on the Liberty Bell. When had the meaning of freedom changed? I wondered. When had employees suddenly become paid volunteers? Of course, nothing had changed except my perceptions. As Hermann Hesse said, admission was simply the price of my mind.

I thought of a Zen retreat I had attended where the teacher recounted the story of her first long retreat. The first day was exciting, she told us. Everything was new, and she was eager to see what it was all about. On the second day the newness was beginning to wear off; restlessness was setting in. By the third day she was seriously doubting the sanity of a person who would spend hours sitting on a meditation cushion when she could be out eating chocolate in the free world. And on day four she woke up cursing at the wake-up gong. "Oh, hell, I *have* to do this," she said out loud, and boom! this became her mantra for the rest of the day.

She knew, however, that if she was going to complete the session, she would have to alter her way of thinking. So on the fifth morning when the gong sounded, instead of complaining that she *had* to do this, she told herself, "I *get* to do this. I get the opportunity to be on this retreat and to learn from what it has to teach." This turned out to be a major turning point for her, not only because she applied it to the retreat, but because she was able to make it an ongoing theme in her personal life as well.

Work can be like this. In the beginning, everything is new and exciting. Then you settle into a comfortable routine. But after a while, if you aren't careful, you may find that routine becoming an "I *have* to do this" situation—a mantra that says you are no longer free.

"I *get* to do this," on the other hand, is the ring of freedom. It's the reminder that you are free to make this choice to be in this particular job at this particular time. It's the opportunity to say, "Okay, maybe this isn't the best job in the universe, but it does support me. It's building my skills so I can move forward."

We have so many choices in the workplace. We are free to

- Appreciate the positives of the situation, rather than focusing on the negatives.
- Encourage supportive relationships that offer an important sense of connection and enhance our days.
- Solve the challenges, rather than perpetuating them by complaining or allowing them to tie us in emotional knots.
- Lighten up and not take our job so seriously that it interferes with the enjoyment of the day.
- View authority figures and policies as guidelines rather than restrictions.
- Seek additional education or training to enable ourselves to advance in our work.

- Give ourselves breaks when we need them . . . take an occasional long lunch hour or an impromptu afternoon at the arboretum or art gallery . . . or even allow ourselves a whole day off once in a while.
- Seek another job when we feel incompatible with a situation, if we have outgrown a position, or if we would simply like to consider new opportunities.

I have also found that I can get a little more freedom into my work by negotiating. Because in the business world a lot more is actually open to negotiation than you think. That is, if you ask.

Although I was unable to negotiate vacation time at the newspaper, I have been free to do so in most of my subsequent situations. For example, I have several times negotiated a new salary level and job title by making a list of my contributions for my employer and pointing out how my efforts will continue to benefit the company. I have negotiated for flex-time, a trade of job duties, and assignment extensions—even in contract jobs where I didn't have long-time rapport. Come to think of it, even some of the inmates I worked with were able to negotiate for privileges through good behavior.

WORK RELEASE

The jail hasn't been my workplace for several years, although I still correspond with inmates who are on work release programs or who are about to be paroled and reenter the workforce. Their letters invariably speak of freedom: comparing the way they saw it before their incarceration and their viewpoints now. A recent letter said, "Having had my liberty taken from me has shown me things which I previously took for granted. It has made me realize that being free without taking unnecessary risks is the real name of the game."

As I read through these letters, they remind me to keep my perspective on freedom. They help me to do my own form of work release in terms of releasing my resistance to a particular colleague or workplace task. They enable me to let go of previous ideas and let in new approaches that will help me to grow. They remind me that no one is commanding me to spin straw into gold, and that even when I have a challenging boss or mountain-heavy deadlines, I have a choice about how much I can handle. If I generally am treated well, experience fulfilling opportunities and make a competitive wage, I can choose to stay. But if the position no longer holds potential on any level, I can choose to move on.

Yes, working with inmates has given me another perspective on freedom in both my work and in my life. It has given me the gift of remembering how many possibilities are available to me and how miraculous it is to be able to choose.

ARE YOU HUMAN BEING,
JOB TITLE—OR BOTH?

EVERYONE CAN relate to the party where you meet someone new and the first question she asks is, "So, what do you do?" Having been through this countless times, you know it doesn't refer to (1) what kind of volunteer work you do; (2) what you do for relaxation on warm summer evenings; or (3) what you do when you find your neighbor's pet boa constrictor slithering up the maple tree outside your front door.

What it does mean, of course, is, "What do you do for a living?" and you are supposed to reply, "I am an electrical engineer" or "I teach second grade" or "I'm in investment banking." The assumption being that the inquisitor will then have a reasonable sense of who you are.

We all know that this is just a conversational lead-in, a sure-fire opener, since most everyone works in some capacity, although I sometimes wonder how this particular question made it to the forefront of introductory etiquette. Is it because we can't think of anything else to say? Is it because we feel we have a sense of a person when we know what he or she "does"? Is it because our internal labeling system feels more comfortable once we know where a person fits in? Probably all of the above. Still, I wonder how much we identify ourselves and each other by our job titles—by what we "do"—and what it really means.

GERMAN HORSE THIEVES AND OTHER IDENTITIES

There is a story in my mother's family that we come from a long line of German horse thieves. According to the story, for generations the family business involved stealing horses, driving them across the border, and selling them in other countries across Europe. No one is sure how it all got started or if it is true, except that stealing horses was apparently part of the family identity. Maybe horse thievery was even in our genes.

As the story goes, someone finally grew tired of the horse business, took a boat to America, and got work as a longshoreman. Other family members followed and found a variety of jobs. Thus, the family identity as horse thieves ended. And, as far as my mother and I know, not one of us has stolen a horse since.

It's true that for many of us our titles are our identity. We are horse thieves or doctors, botanists or alligator wrestlers; our professions simply chose us at birth. The job descended upon us as the family business, or through karma, or through an overwhelming drive, and presto! here we are. For instance, I met a woman who identified so strongly with her poetry that she introduced herself as "Chloe, a poet." The words shot out of her mouth without a thought. And I knew a man who had "Entrepreneur" following his name on his letterhead, although no one knew what he actually did. Then there is the graphic designer I worked with a few years ago who reminded his colleagues ad nauseam that he was an *Art*-ist.

All of these people were their titles; their titles were themselves. For other folks, their backgrounds, talents, and interests are completely different from their titles. Take my friend Jon, for example. Ask him at a party what he does and he will say, "Projectionist." Yes, his day job—or night job, literally—is running the projection booth at an art cinema. He enjoys the work, it pays the bills, and he gets to see a lot of good films in the process. But mostly what Jon does is ants. Seriously—ants. Several thousand a week. He keeps ant farms all over his house and spends his days studying their behavior, charting their patterns, writing out observations. For Jon, movies pay his way, but entomology is his really-o, truly-o work.

My friend Tina's real work also doesn't correspond with her title. Currently seeking a position in linguistics, she has taken interim jobs as telemarketer and word processor. So if you saw her at the hors d'oeuvres table and inquired about her job, her response wouldn't tell you much about who she really is. Rather, you would have a more interesting conversation if you knew that Tina has a black belt in aikido; that she is fluent in five languages, including Ukrainian; that she teaches ESL classes one night a week, has studied Japanese culture in Kyoto in exchange for giving English and French lessons, and has traveled through half of the world.

Despite the fact that people often have so much going on in their lives beyond their jobs, in our society we are fascinated by titles. Everything has to have a label. Indeed, I even met a miniature poodle named Muffy who had a title. Muffy "worked" in an assisted care facility and wore a little red badge that said, "Registered Assistance Dog." I'll admit it was very cute, but it did remind me that titles, like beauty, only go so deep.

KEEPING TITLES IN PERSPECTIVE

When I was thirteen, I had the pleasure of spending an evening with Dr. Louis Leakey, who was visiting a friend's father, an archaeology professor at Cornell University. In my mind, it was an enjoyable visit with a white-haired gentleman who treated me like an adult and played with my friend's Siamese kitten Peter. When I mentioned to my friend that I thought Dr. Leakey was a very nice man, she sniffed disgustedly, "No, he isn't, dummy! Don't you know anything? He's a *famous paleontologist.*"

There is no doubt that, from a practical standpoint, titles serve a vital purpose. They are effective for providing a match-up of individuals with the work they perform, so we can easily locate an individual who can supply the product or service we need. Let's face it, if you need a famous paleontologist for a project, a marine architect isn't going to fit the bill. And when your car needs fixing and your faucet is leaking, respectively you want a mechanic and a plumber. If titles were nonexistent, how would you know how to find the right person for the job?

On a more personal level, titles are useful for identifying our skills and building our careers. They are stepping-stones to more advanced positions, front-row tickets to professional success.

Like anything else in life, however, titles tend to take over if we don't keep them in perspective. They become monsters if we grant them too much importance, or if we "fall too hard for our own publicity clippings," as author Anne Lamott says. A good case in point is the *Art*-ist I mentioned earlier. He waded so deeply into his clippings that he began to object to all but the most creative aspects of his job. He complained that it was beneath him to type copy or scan photos. He would work only with select clients; after all, he was an *Art*-ist, and he thought he should have only the best.

Meanwhile, his coworkers, also artists, had to take up the slack, and they felt resentful. And the *Art*-ist's select clients began to avoid him, preferring to work with other staff members who were more pleasant and flexible about their needs. Eventually word got to the top. And when his company played its next round of corporate musical chairs, guess whose seat was the first to go when the music stopped?

Titles can also haunt us in a different way if we allow them to gnaw at our self-esteem or our self-respect because we feel we should be something more. I recall a corporate receptionist who hung her head in shame, feeling that she was the lowest on the business totem pole. In her mind, everyone else had a more serious job. They made real contributions to the business, while all she did was answer the phone. Little did she realize how much she contributed with her cheerful smile and her heartfelt concern. Or how important her work really was, since she created the company's first impression—the impression that can be so crucial to professional success.

Chögyam Trungpa said, "Whether you are a gas station attendant or the president of your country doesn't matter. When you experience the goodness of being alive, you can respect who and what you are." We typically think of our work as defining us, but, in truth, aren't we the ones who shape a job? Isn't it we, and not the job, who are so very much alive? After all, every position, every title, begins with a living, breathing human being who has built up a unique collection of qualities and life experiences. A human being who has been in existence for several years prior to entering the workplace. So a title can't exactly define who we are. But we can, as Meister Eckhart said, "ennoble our works." We can bring our best selves to the fore and make an enormous difference to the situation, whatever the job.

TITLES AS LURES

My friend Kathy says that job titles and job descriptions are some of the best accidental fiction she has ever come across. I tend to agree. Sometimes I peruse the classifieds to see what the employment gods are currently serving up, and what I've seen lately is a trend toward creative job titles. For example, a person who works for a trash service is called a sanitation specialist; an administrative assistant is a member of professional staff; a woman who stays home to raise her children is called a domestic engineer; and an employee of a submarine sandwich shop is called a sub artist. And so forth and so on. Accidental fiction or not?

An advertisement that recently caught my eye was an opening for a pet counselor. After imagining my Jungian alter ego, notepad in hand, encouraging a springer spaniel to get in touch with his inner puppy, my more skeptical self called the number in the ad and asked for a job description. I was told that the counselor sells sundry pet products, runs the cash register, cleans cages, exercises the animals, and, incidentally, disseminates information about pets, which made up the "counseling" aspect of the work.

Such titles draw applicants who are attracted to something more interesting than the usual humdrum positions—and heck, shouldn't work be more exciting? Shouldn't we all have more creative titles? But job seekers should beware that the actual responsibilities may not exactly match the title presented. Because jargon runs rampant in the employment world, like everywhere else. In my experience, "specialist" often refers to a catch-all generalist, "counselor" is frequently used to describe someone who works in sales or cleans up after others, and "artist" may very well refer to someone who slaps something—not necessarily art— together. Of course, these titles could also be the real thing, but it's important to read between the lines (and ask the employer a lot of questions) to find out how well the title fits the actual job.

Though some of these titles may initially help people to feel better about their work, this practice can also be an employer's manipulative way of luring higher-skilled candidates into lower-level jobs. I've seen it time and time again. The employer embellishes a job description because she wants to lure the cream of the crop. This usually works in that it nets a number of candidates with more advanced skills than she needs. During the interview, when the real description becomes evident, the employer explains that there is "potential" for advancement. In other words, while the employee can't actually expect to perform the advertised responsibilities at first, they *may* be added in the future. Sometimes the employer is telling the truth; other times she just wants a highly skilled warm body to fill the slot.

I knew a woman, desperate to escape the secretarial profession, who fell into one such job. Pleased to be called a project administrator rather than a secretary, she launched cheerfully into the work, only to discover that the title was a nice way to describe sweeping up the crumbs of everyone else's creative work. Instead of having specific duties, she was on perpetual call to deal with her colleagues' last-minute pieces. This was worse, in her opinion, than her previous secretarial position, where at least she had her own job. Unfortunately for both employer and employee, the situation lasted only three months, after which they both had to begin the search/hire process again. Does anyone ever win when the job isn't honestly defined?

Where am I going with this? Am I trying to say that titles serve a certain purpose, but they are relative, after all? Am I trying to redefine my own work in terms of what I have to give, instead of being confined to the limitations of what I'm called? Am I questioning whether a particular title is really going to give anyone the full satisfaction they need? I guess I'm trying to say all of the above. I also hope the next time my neighbor's boa constrictor slithers up my maple tree, I will attend a party and someone will say "reptilian rescue representative" when I sidle up to him and pointedly ask, "What do you do?"

UNUSUAL ROUTES
TO THE TOP

E VERYONE LOVES a success story, and I know several. Consider Lee, who lost his job as a geologist when the bottom dropped out of the oil industry several years back. Because he had five children to support, he needed work fast, so he accepted the first full-time position he could find—driving a city bus. Although he had to adjust to ever-changing hours, difficult passengers, and the monotony of driving the same route every day, he gave it his all and worked to develop patience, flexibility, a sense of responsibility for the safety of his passengers, and a sense of humor about his job—all challenging tasks that eventually he was pleased to be able to master.

Even so, Lee knew he couldn't drive a bus for the rest of his life. Nor was he certain how soon he might find another geology position, so he decided to pursue his longtime interest in applying to the foreign service. Aware that it might take years of study to pass the rigorous tests and that he might not even be accepted, he nevertheless took his pursuit seriously (at one point he had eighty books checked out from the public library). Seven years later he realized his goal. He is now vice consul for an embassy in one of the Baltic states—and is on his way to the top.

Now consider Audra, who made her living as a receptionist for a research firm while working toward her lifelong dream of being a primatologist in Africa. Although she already had a degree in biology and had taken a trip to Rwanda after college, she realized that she needed to fill additional requirements in order to meet her goal. Uncertain of what these requirements were, she contacted several gorilla foundations as well as renowned experts in the field. Many of them offered important insights and helped her execute her plans. Next she set herself on a personal program of (1) obtaining an advanced degree; (2) learning wildlife photography basics; (3) taking a short leave of absence from her job to take another trip to Africa; and (4) establishing contacts with the primate advocacy group she hoped to join.

Meanwhile, Audra cheerfully persevered through ringing telephones, rejection letters, and well-meaning friends and co-workers who tried to discourage her from what they regarded as an impossible scheme. Imagine their surprise when, after four years, her hard work paid off. The last I saw her, Audra had given the research firm two weeks' notice and was packing for the job of her dreams.

ALLOW THE DREAM TO HAPPEN

John Gardner, the late novelist and author of books on writing, said, "To really write one must allow the dream to happen." Although these words were directed toward aspiring writers, they can certainly apply to anything one yearns to do. Joining the foreign service. Becoming a primatologist in Africa. Long-distance running. Fashion photography. Whatever. The advice is for the taking, if you are willing to give it a chance.

I meet people all the time who want to be writers, but they can't seem to find the time to write. Yes, I know it would be infinitely easier if there were a hundred more hours in a day. And yes, it would be more feasible if there weren't so many blasted things to do. Still, if you want to be a writer, stop telling yourself that you *want* to be a writer and *be* a writer instead. Ignore the fact that life is roaring eighty miles an hour around your head, step off the fast track for a while, and make a date with your creative self to do the work.

It gives you a head start when you take your dream seriously. When you agree with yourself that this is a priority, no matter what your friends, coworkers, Aunt Medusa, Cousin Wolfgang, or anyone else thinks. It also helps to act while your aspirations are fresh and your energy is high and to take small steps toward your goal. Sit down with pen and paper. Make a few phone calls to inquire about classes, applications, volunteer programs, or anything else you need to do. Make more phone calls. Take that class or fill out the proper application. Because once you actually start the process and make a commitment to yourself to stay with it, you have already made a lot of progress toward realizing your dream.

My friend Mike took his first step toward the top by committing to write each evening after dinner, five nights a week. His pact with his creative spirit was to write for at least thirty minutes or to produce one vignette, whichever came first. Some nights he kept to the half hour. Other nights he found himself scribbling into the witching hour. Either way, he didn't worry about editing as he went. He just wrote. He didn't worry about the vignettes turning into a book, or about the book sitting on a bookstore shelf. He just wrote. He ignored the temptation to imagine the book turning into such a smash success that he could quit his day job, make multiple publicity appearances, live off the enormous royalty checks, and write his heart out into the sunset. He just wrote. And wrote. And wrote.

Within several months Mike had a series of pieces that he gave as "gift readings" to his friends. Although the vignettes didn't grow into a book, eventually a few of them were published in literary magazines, which gave him considerable momentum to continue. Mike says he has his writing sessions to thank for this because they loosened up his thoughts, helped him to work out the kinks in his rhythms, and taught him to write more quickly and easily. The sessions also taught him to just keep going, no matter what. At this writing, he is up to two hours a day, working on a psychothriller.

The same principle applies to any dream—social work, aerobics instruction, desktop publishing, anything. Even if you don't have the time or finances to go back to school right now . . . even if your current job takes up a lot of time . . . even if your life seems to be an endless series of unedited run-on sentences and you see a loooooooong road ahead, you can still be seriously involved with your dreams in small ways. You can volunteer a few hours a week through your county social service agency. Or set up an aerobics program at work and offer lunch-hour classes to fellow employees. You can seek out others who have a similar dream by joining a writing group or taking a desktop publishing class through a community extension program. You can align yourself with professionals who offer advice and support. Even if you only have one extra hour a day, you can focus on giving it your all during that short period.

You might even take a job that has flexible hours, leaving key hours free to pursue your dream. I know people who cleaned houses or offices while working toward their goals—among them a yoga teacher, a gerontologist, an acupuncturist, and a psychotherapist. These folks cleaned around their classes, supported themselves while gaining valuable experience, and experienced the considerable benefits, as one man explained, of having solitary time to think, plus on-the-job exercise. They have all moved fulltime into their chosen careers.

Whatever time you can spare, by acting on your dreams you keep them alive.

TIME TRAVELING

Do you remember the *Calvin and Hobbes* comic strip in which Calvin tries to avoid writing his school paper by boarding a time machine and traveling into the future? His strategy is that by the time he returns, he will have completed and presented the paper, leaving him to move on to bigger and better things. I attempted the same plan when writing this book, to no avail. When it came down to it, both Calvin and I had to hunker down and do the job.

One way to realize your dreams is to view yourself as traveling through time. That is, to consider where you want to be in a year (or two or five) and then looking at the time you will travel through to get there—including now. Now is a great and powerful tool because it is something that we all have in abundance as we pursue our dreams. It may not look like much at first, but think about it: now becomes tomorrow, which becomes the next day, which turns into next week. Next week turns into next month and subsequently next year. As you travel through each day, you exert a little more effort toward your goal, learning what you can. Finally, you have traveled through so much time that your dream is here. Yes, that dream is now.

Beyond your personal efforts, in traveling day to day, you also learn valuable skills that can be useful in your dreams of the future. Through an ordinary job such as driving a bus, you might understand something important about human behavior that you can later apply to the foreign service (and have plenty of time and incentive left over to study for the exams). Through routine receptionist work, you may develop a sense of spontaneity and organization that would be an asset anywhere, including the African bush.

The beauty of time travel is that you can always expect the unexpected. You never know when you will discover an opportunity this afternoon via an activity that you're engaged in this morning, or when a person you meet today will be your dream contact of tomorrow. When I first went freelance with my writing, I did a fair amount of temporary work to fill in the financial gaps. Though I was initially resistant to some of my assignments, I came to appreciate what they taught me—flexibility, communication skills with a wider range of individuals, self-reliance—and I even

came to write a book about it. Traveling through the temporary
employment realm became an integral part of my writing career
and thus played a large part in realizing my goal.

DIFFERENT PEOPLE, DIFFERENT ROUTES

It's sometimes a challenge to look at the people who are successful
in the area toward which you are striving and not think, "Why
can't that be me?" After all, you've worked your —— off, you've
made the contacts, you've bent over backwards and stood on your
head at all the right times and in all the right places. Furthermore,
you are intelligent, talented, sensitive, and gorgeous, too. So why
did they get there instead of you?

What we all tend to forget during these moments of comparing ourselves to Ms. Super Achiever or Mr. Top-o'-the-Mountain
is that we are all different human beings. We are on our own
schedules, with different routes. Some of us have routes that take
us more directly to our goals, while others have longer, rockier,
more roundabout trails. Some have whole mountain ranges or
oceans to cross, whereas others just have a skip and a jump. Why
that is, I don't know. But look at Christopher Columbus, who
actually missed his mark by thousands of miles when he landed
in North America. And Thomas Edison, who is known for a few
famous inventions, although most of his efforts didn't achieve the
same level of success. Then there is Henry David Thoreau, whose
initial publication of *Walden* was so badly received that the majority of the first edition ended up in the author's private library. It's
incredible to imagine when you consider how we still draw on
this significant book today.

Some people are late bloomers like the saguaro cactus, which
flowers for the first time in its fiftieth year. My mother had a
friend who worked as a directory assistance operator for thirty
years before pursuing the education she needed to teach in an
Appalachian mountain school. I worked with a man who became

an attorney after retiring from a lifetime career as a corporate financial analyst. Not to mention several others I know who went from administrators to law enforcement officers, scientists to massage therapists, and even a monk who gave up the cloth for mystery novel writing—all later in life.

And why not bloom late? Why not be like Grandma Moses, who didn't begin painting until she was in her late seventies, was still at it when she turned one hundred, and created more than a thousand paintings before she died? It's never too late to begin realizing our dreams.

Sometimes our route is not only roundabout, but it seems to take us backwards instead. One professional couple I met found themselves in serious auto reverse and landed in a city homeless shelter. Through a series of personal misfortunes, they both lost their advertising jobs and subsequently their house. It was certainly a terrifying time until they were able to find full-time employment and another home for themselves and their teenage daughter. Nevertheless, as they later realized, the situation opened them up for a whole new awareness that would have eluded them had they continued in their previous breakneck speed. It allowed them to slow down and gradually move out of their well-known grooves to pursue a new direction.

"Hitting rock bottom almost devastated us, but it was also a wake-up call," they told me. "It made us realize that we had just taken too many risks at once, had allowed too many others to make decisions for us and that we needed to take better charge of our lives. We started seeing a Methodist counselor, and we're beginning to understand that having a fulfilling job and money in the bank are goals to work toward, but they aren't all that holds us together. When we look at family and God as our top priorities, we realize that we have a strong base to build on."

It's unlikely that most of us will find our route through a homeless shelter. But, whatever your route, just keep going. If you don't meet a goal right away, remember that the road between aspiration and achievement is a few miles long and it takes some time to get there. Okay, maybe Ms. Super Achiever got there first. So maybe she has been traveling longer than you. Or maybe she drives her career way past the normal speed limit. But forget about all that right now. Instead, concentrate on what is really important—you. Then ask yourself:

- Are my expectations realistic?
- Am I seriously concentrating on where I want to go, or do I give up too easily?
- Instead of setting impossibly long-reaching goals, can I create shorter goals that offer small successes?
- Am I giving the dream a serious chance?

Remind yourself of how far you've already traveled, appreciate yourself for your efforts, and try to work one day at a time to create your own story of success. I have taped a little *I Ching* wisdom to my computer to serve this purpose: "Do not think about the gains you might make or the possible setbacks that could befall you. Continue in righteous progress and you will be blessed with good fortune."

Chances are, you probably will.

Getting
By

THE CHARACTERS
IN THE ELEVATOR

I ALWAYS think of the work community as my favorite kind of story: "the characters in the elevator." This is the story in which a group of very different people crowd into the elevator of a tall building, and the elevator has a l-o-n-g ride up or, better yet, gets stuck between floors. The characters, their heads full of their personal agendas, their great big plans, must then relate to one another within that small square of space, within that small square of time. With diverse personalities and backgrounds, and maybe speaking several different languages, they have to find ways to communicate and work toward a common goal—even if that goal is only to scream "Heeeeeeelp!" in Swahili and hope the elevator gods will hear their plea.

In this kind of story, by the time the doors are opened, the characters are changed, if only a little. It is like the children's book by Leo Lionni where Little Blue meets Little Yellow, they touch, and each becomes a little green. By the time the characters in the elevator emerge, they have tinted each other ever so slightly. They have become a little of each other on a certain level. Some have exchanged life stories. Some have each other's telephone numbers. A few hate each other's guts. Others seem unaffected, although they are obviously relieved to escape the claustrophobic space and humdrum music. Whatever they take from the experience, most have new insights to carry along on their life journey. Insights that somehow alter their views on work and life, even if they never step into another elevator again.

The workplace is like that: a great collective of characters of various ages and genders and personalities and backgrounds. An assembly of colleagues in all shapes and sizes and colors and titles—and, at times, their alter egos, too. Some are madly traditional, others unconventional. Some are, well, simply characters. And, like the elevator cast, there they all are. In it. Together. In a particular space. Having to work toward a common goal.

Of course, if you have a regular job, you know the characters in your particular elevator. You have a general sense of who these people are and what they might do next. But on any given day, you never know exactly which ones will be along for the ride or what kind of chemistry they will create. Today's combination may include

- A production meeting of the editorial director, Ezekiel Rumpletoff, and the artist who draws purple lions and green tigers on her shaven head.
- A noontime conference of yourself (fortified by your daily lunch of tofu paté and carrot sticks), the enigmatic editor-at-large who is usually traveling around the world, and the man from payroll who warns you daily that people who eat carrots eventually die.
- The ever-stylish art director, your assistant who makes you clean up your desk, and the marketing VP with the contagious laugh.
- An informal meeting with the office muses, who sometimes leave spiritual books on your chair.

Or perhaps it's just you and the pointy-haired Boss from Hell, discussing your weekly status report. Oh, grooooooooooooooan.

What I like about applying the characters-in-the-elevator story to the workplace is that it increases the odds, dresses up the day a bit more, extends the possibilities. It encourages a stronger connection with colleagues and offers the realization that you receive something useful in every exchange. For instance, Monday's meeting may inspire you to be more creative—although you may not go so far as drawing animals on your head (or anywhere else). Tuesday may find you wanting to know more about the inscrutable characters and taking others with a grain of carrot-colored salt. Wednesday may have you spiffing up your wardrobe and organizing your office, while Thursday has you laughing more. And Friday you might be concerned with more creative and spiritual issues, which is fortunate since creativity and compassion are imperative when staring into the ever-beady eyes of the Boss from Hell.

Whatever the combination, however it inspires you, every situation is bound to be . . . shall we say *interesting*? to say the least. With some give and take, some push and pull, some wild chemistry—and perhaps a teensy hint of alchemy, too. There may even be smoke, as the time Valerie's coworker accidentally set her long blonde hair on fire with a lighter and another colleague doused it with his ginseng Coke.

Another thing I like about the characters-in-the-elevator story is how it plays into the workplace social network, delving into the personal interactions that happen at work. After all, do you think those characters are just hanging out in the elevator, having one business meeting after another? Scribbling equations on the proverbial white board, passing around perfect-bound annual reports, la-dee-dah, ho-hum? Of course not. Between the equations, the tedious reports, they are also getting to know one another on a personal level. One person is describing the great blue heron he saw in flight on his way to the office that morning. Someone is listening intently as a colleague tells how she almost rode off a cliff on her mountain bike vacation in Moab. Someone else says, "Hey, I'm starving. Anyone up for Japanese takeout?" And another replies, "Put me down for California roll and octopus when we get out of here."

Through these exchanges, the characters not only establish rapport, but they are going beyond being individual characters to being parts of the group. They are enhancing communication, support, trust, respect—qualities that increase productivity, motivation, and a collective push toward the common goal. They are forming important human bonds that also cement the work.

At some point, one of those elevator characters might do something to touch you in such a way that you will remember years later. This happened to me during a publishing job I had in Boston. That year I was reading *Light Years* by James Salter. Besides enjoying the poetic writing ("Life is weather. Life is meals. Lunches on a blue checked cloth on which salt has spilled. . . ."), I wondered about a mysterious liqueur that the characters were drinking—something called San Raphael. Oh, I knew that San Raphael was a city somewhere, but I didn't know the drink. It sounded so exotic that I asked around the office to find out if anyone knew what it was, if anyone had tasted it. But no one had.

After savoring *Light Years* for weeks (it was one of those books I didn't want to finish), I finally forced myself to read the last page, which was as poignant as I had expected. Then I went on with my life of weather and meals and forgot all about it.

Weeks later, I returned from a meeting and found a bottle on my desk from a coworker. A bottle of red-colored liqueur called San Raphael. As it was a late Friday afternoon, I opened it and served cups to everyone. As I recall, it was rather like a syrupy port, a little sweet. At any rate, the San Raphael was gone within minutes and my mystery was solved. But the thoughtfulness of that elevator character remains an experience I still remember fondly.

DIFFICULT CHARACTERS

There are undoubtedly a few other characters you will recollect for a long time, too. Characters you remember all too well. They are the ones who get on your nerves, drive you crazy, upset you no end. The ones who push your buttons all at once, including a few you didn't know you had. They are the characters about whom you groan, How did this person get into my elevator, anyway? Who let him onto this planet . . . into my workplace . . . into *my life*?

Ah, me. I've had several of those myself.

Fortunately, the majority of us work in offices larger than the average elevator—otherwise the prisons would undoubtedly be more overcrowded than they already are. Still, when it comes to difficult people, even the World Trade Center isn't spacious enough. But what can you do? With such a wide range of personalities within a single workplace, there will always be a few challenging ones.

Simone Weil said, "It is good to reflect about whatever forces us to come out of ourselves." I always think of this when faced with a difficult colleague because that person forces me out of myself all right—if only to reflect on my murderous thoughts. Okay, murder is a bit extreme; let's say I would be relieved to astral-project that colleague to Pluto; then I could have some peace and quiet. So far, this hasn't worked, however. Inevitably, I open my eyes to realize that this person not only still exists but is *expanding* within my space.

This happened to me not too long ago. I was doing some contract work at Company X when I found myself dealing with *one of those*: a woman who was extremely territorial about her work space and reluctant to share the project work with me, even though she clearly needed help. After attempting in vain to wish her into hyperspace, I finally took a step back and had a good long look at the situation. Which brought me to the realization that this wasn't just about her; it was also about me. Uh-oh time. It was apparent that I was going to have to do some shadow work again.

There are times when I see the things I need to work on in myself by what annoys me the most in my colleagues—by what gets on my nerves and in my face. Through recognizing what Carl Jung called the shadow side, I see the aspects of myself that I don't like or don't want to acknowledge—aspects that can help me take a step toward self-understanding in the workplace. In this particular case, as I grew more and more irritated with my colleague at Company X, I saw myself shadowboxing. That is, I saw the same shadows in me that I didn't like in her: wanting to be in control, not wanting to share the work or my space.

Of course, I didn't want this revelation. No, I would have preferred to bask in my own perfection and blame everything on her. Or to astral-project her to Pluto, take over the project, and get it done my own sweet way, avoiding the issue altogether. But once I saw what I was up against, I had no choice but to accept my shadow side. At which point I was able to take a few deep breaths, accept my imperfections, and let them go—if only just a little. Then I could get on to the important task of doing the work.

Besides showing you your shadow, difficult characters may turn out to be catalysts for a great turn of events. Once my friend Anne had a personality conflict with a supervisor on a temporary clerical assignment in a large corporation. She had been unhappy with the situation for several weeks but was just riding it out until the assignment ended. Eventually she became so frustrated that hanging on was clearly an impossibility. So she walked across the building to another department, where she spoke with a woman she had briefly worked with the year before.

The result? The woman Anne spoke with needed someone right away to do some writing, which was Anne's chosen field, so she was able to end her unpleasant assignment and move into a preferable situation. Not only that, but it turned out to be one of the most meaningful jobs she ever had, with people she really enjoyed. *And* it opened up a series of subsequent writing projects. All because of a disagreeable character who inadvertently nudged her to move on.

Sometimes a difficult character is someone who doesn't understand you or your situation. This happened to me on one job.

A man in my department frequently walked by my desk, never approached, never spoke, but always looked me in the eye and frowned. At first I thought he might be shy, so I tried to be pleasant. To no avail. He continued to be silent, to frown.

After a while I grew uncomfortable, even a little paranoid. Was there something wrong with the way I dressed? Was I doing something seriously offensive? Or worse, maybe he was an ax murderer in disguise, with plans to attack me as I left the office one night.

Finally I couldn't stand it any longer and I confronted him. I found out someone told him I had written a book called *Temp*, but he had heard the title as *Pimp*. And he just didn't like the idea of sharing his particular elevator with "that kind of girl."

One of the great things about the workplace is that it exposes us to so many other people, difficult characters and all. This is one reason that, although I often write at home, I also enjoy working in an office. For one thing, I couldn't work alone all the time; I'm more of a social kind of cat. Second, I love the characters-in-the-elevator story, and I don't have enough multiple personalities to generate a good handful of characters on my own. Also, I usually find that I have more in common with most people than I expect, that we all want the same basic things from a job, and this is always a pleasant surprise.

Sure, some days are up and down. Other days I wish I could get off on a different floor. But mostly, I appreciate my co-characters for enriching the ride.

Some of my real-life colleagues have been actual elevator characters: a man who shared a freshly steamed artichoke with me in a New York skyscraper; a Colorado businessman who is a suspect in a world-famous murder case; and a dog trainer who was taking ten black poodles on red leashes to a groomer on the top floor of a London professional building.

Recently, I was in an office elevator when I heard a deep, disembodied voice speaking in a language I didn't understand.

Certain that I had been the only person to board the elevator, I quickly looked around. Yes, I was the only passenger, so where was this voice coming from? Another voice appeared, in the same language. Was it Portuguese? Urdu? Swahili? Were they the elevator gods?

I soon discovered that two men were deep inside the elevator, making repairs. They were real workers in a real workplace. They were not the characters of some crazy author's analogy. Being characters in the elevator was actually their job.

A JOB WITH A VIEW

WHETHER OUR job is writing, teaching, running a cash register in a zoological bookstore, or being a character in an elevator, we need to find some creativity in our work. Yes, once in a while—on alternate Tuesdays, perhaps—we need to meet the part of us that is capable of opening the drapes, looking out the window, and taking in a larger view. Considering, for a few moments, the binoculars if we are used to the microscope . . . the larger picture if we are used to the printed page . . . or the magnifying glass if we are used to the telescope. If we can go outside of ourselves and look at our situation in a different light, we can begin to see a world of creativity in our current work. We can begin to create a job with a view.

We tend to think of creativity as something grandiose—the ability to produce an ingenious musical composition, an enormous mural, or a best-selling novel—but it is actually closer to us than that. After all, to be human is to have the ability to create; we are inherently creative no matter what we do. True, some of us have more imaginative work than others, but at our root we all have the capacity for some form of imagination. We have only to remember to think of ourselves as inventive, to realize that we *can* offer more creativity to our work.

Shunryu Suzuki said, "True being comes out of nothingness, moment after moment. Nothingness is always there, and from it everything appears." Creativity is like this. It begins with a chunk of what we initially see as nothingness: a solid white canvas, a blank piece of paper, a gray ho-hum Monday morning. It begins with our basic, everyday selves operating within the space that is this moment. Creativity begins with—and evolves from—a willingness to work with what we have. We don't have to wait for something monumental to happen—the dream job, the winning lottery ticket, the perfect relationship, divine inspiration. We have the basic tools we need right here, right now.

Take something as mundane as the objects on your desk. By viewing them from a different angle, you may be able to see something beautiful in the round alabaster vase filled with colored pens, the pink seashell your friend Amelie brought back from Greece, the sandhill cranes flying across your deskside calendar.

Take something as usual as your coworker at the next workstation. By entertaining the possibility that she is more than remotely interesting, you might begin to enjoy the fact that her hazel eyes sparkle when she laughs, that she always wears jade dragons on her left ear, that she has a piece of real toast suspended over her desk to indicate her membership in Toastmasters. From here you might change perspective on the rest of your routine—the weekly staff meeting, the daily reports, the same old telephone calls. You might find yourself taking a break from your automatic responses and opening up to the freshness of the day.

The world is full of jobs that we don't typically consider creative, full of people doing these jobs. The philosopher and spiritual writer Simone Weil worked for many years as a laborer on farms and in automobile factories. The author Peter Matthiessen once made his living as a longshoreman. Both developed an appreciation for the mechanics of this manual labor as they worked and were able to incorporate their experiences into later creative works.

Similarly, I had a friend who stocked produce in a small neighborhood market in Greenwich Village. His job was to transfer fruits and vegetables from crates to counters all day, every day. He could have focused on the monotony of the work, just lining up the produce hour after hour, oh yawn, ho-hum. Instead, he chose to view the fruits and vegetables as a wonderful parade of colors, shapes, and textures. He chose to consider their colorful names as short, bright poems: asPARagus, CAULiflower, ARTichoke, UGlifruit. KohlRAbi. ShiiTAKi MUSHroom. And in doing so, he discovered creativity in the nitty-gritty of the daily grind.

Okay, I admit some days are a serious challenge. Some days the nitty-gritty stares you down and dares you to wallow in its ominous depths. On these days the burlap walls of your small office seem to grow grayer every minute, you don't feel the least bit motivated by the project that just crept across your desk, and you're sure there is potentially hazardous mold growing on your colleague's hanging toast. On these days, no way is routine work creative. No way, no how, are vegetables poetry. Everything is dulldulldull.

If you are like me, you can handle a single day like this, maybe even a stoic few. But after a while it just gets old. At some point the dullness gets damnably boring. So what do you do? "There are two clear options," a colleague suggested when I posed this question. "Get creative or eat the toast."

EDITORIALIZE

Journalist Robert Wieder said of his own work, "The creative person looks for history in a hardware store and fashion in an airport." In other words, the creative person seeks innovation wherever he goes. With this in mind, consider the media. Newspapers, magazines, television, and radio are full of commentaries about people in all kinds of jobs, including your own. They are usually employees who approach their work in a way that gives the story a special twist. Let's say this employee is you, which isn't as far-fetched as you might think. So . . . if a journalist came to your company to interview you, what about your work would make a story? Do you perform it with a flair that is an inspiration to others? Do you offer a new take on an age-old profession? Do you have the jump on an emerging technology? Whatever you do, there is a certain quality that *you* bring to this work. What is the twist?

DRAMATIZE

Now leap onto the white stage of your mind. Yes, I know this is slightly dramatic, but indulge yourself for just a moment. No one is watching, I guarantee. Sit still for a few minutes and fill this stage-mind with your job. Consider the positives that draw you to the office day after day. Conjure up the simple pleasures that you experience as you sit at your desk. Get down to the teensy-weensy details: the color of the tools you use to do your work (in my case, a rainbow assortment of fine-point pens), the time and texture of your next deadline, the screech-owl call you received this morning from your most demanding client. Hold these thoughts for a full minute (tick, tick, tick).

Okay, time's up. Time to change into something fancy and go to a party. Any party, anywhere. You pick. The gala could be in Paris or Rio de Janeiro. It could be on top of the Taj Mahal. Anyway, go there. Imagine yourself standing by the hors d'oeuvres table, sipping a glass of something expensive when someone *very* interesting-looking appears and asks, in a heart-stopping Italian accent, what you do for a living. First glance says you want to talk to this person for the rest of your life. First thought says you better make yourself (and your job) sound like a world-class event. How are you going to meet the challenge?

VISUALIZE

Next sift through your employment history and make a list of the top ten most unusual things that ever happened to you at work. Your work history is probably a greater collective of creative incidents than you realize. These events don't necessarily have to fit within the framework of your job description. In fact, they probably don't. They are more likely the little frills with which we employees decorate our ragged souls as we attempt to make an honest living. They are the stories we find ourselves telling again and again and again.

When my friend Hannah did this exercise she remembered the time she played the messages on the office answering machine and the whole tape was filled with someone's barking dog. Next she recalled the year she worked in a voodoo shop during college when a large African mask fell off the wall onto her head during a thunderstorm. Fortunately, she only received a scratch and the gods were thereafter silent, but it sure made for some good spontaneous excitement. And it's a story that has kept its drama over the years.

Consider the creative events that scream out between the lines of your work. The incidents and people that have offered unexpected entertainment beyond the job. Have you ever answered a colleague's telephone and found yourself talking to a long-lost friend whom you knew in a different city two decades ago? Did you ever discover a mysterious scroll on your chair that read, "Forget work. Let's run away together," as once happened to me? What extra thrills punctuate your life and hence your career? To help stimulate your memory, here is my own true-to-life list compiled from several years of different work experiences.

- I'm designing a poster at a high-tech company. A woman in a short black dress and red high heels walks into my office, bearing a foot-high chocolate tyrannosaurus rex. She quickly breaks off the head and offers it to me.
- I'm coordinating a conference at an atmospheric research center when a dark-bearded man appears in the hallway, looks deeply into my eyes, and recites several Shakespearean sonnets in a British accent with perfect cadence.

- A man delivering photocopies to me gets stuck in the elevator of the large office building. The alarm sounds. The rescue squad arrives: a fire truck and an ambulance. Everyone in the adjacent offices stops work and runs into the hallway. We all cheer when the character in the elevator is finally free.
- I'm laying out a page at the newspaper of my first job when I hear a great bout of shouting. I look up in time to see a very large editor pick up a very large trash barrel and throw it across the room.
- I'm on a contract assignment for a company that manufactures robots. During the course of a single week, I meet an engineer who, at her desk, nurses injured animals back to health for the local humane society; FedEx shirts and underwear to the vice president, whose business trip lasts longer than expected; and am invited, over lunch hour, to watch a videotape of a coworker's gallbladder operation (I politely decline).
- I'm working at home on a newsletter for a historic preservation group when there is a knock at the door. It is a young photo intern who always danced in the newsroom at my first job and later ran off to Rhodesia to become a mercenary. Now he is back, wanting to talk and asking if I will teach him yoga.
- I'm sitting at a tilted light table, viewing slides in the production department of a publishing company. My back is to the door. Suddenly there is a sound of chanting behind me and a freak hailstorm inside the room. It takes me a while to realize that a Tibetan spiritual leader has blessed the room with a prayer and a handful of (uncooked) white rice.
- I'm teaching preschool. In a creative drama exercise, a fellow teacher turns thirty children into wild animals but doesn't know how to turn them back into children again. The entire school is on safari, on their hands and knees, screeching, roaring, climbing the walls. We have to figure out how to turn them all back into children again.
- After-hours on a publication job, I roll a blank sheet of paper into a colleague's typewriter and type a single sentence. The

next day the sheet is back in my typewriter with a paragraph added. We volley like this for weeks until we have a completed a very bizarre story. Ten years and many jobs later, a similar volley continues with the same person via E-mail.

- I'm at work in my study when I hear a ruckus downstairs. I go down to investigate, find the aftermath on the floor, and see that the cat has eaten a whole bear.

We can't always be fountains of creativity, but it will give our work more life if sometimes we find a different perspective. If we exaggerate just a little. If once in a while we take the view that the cat didn't just eat an animal cracker—he ate *a whole bear.*

Oh, some days we might have to stimulate ourselves by making lists or bringing a jar of sunflowers and calypso music into the workplace, or by seeking out a colleague whose priority is *fun.* Other days we might do something a little different, like turn our schedules upside down or bring our children (or a friend's children) to work for a day. When Hannah did this she got—besides peanut butter and jelly on her computer keyboard—a sense of wonderment about her job that was a pleasant surprise.

On occasion it may help to leave the office early, go into the city, and expose yourself to some creativity at large. Build up your momentum by viewing an art film or seeing your friend Carrie's stellar performance in *Egad! The Woman in White.* Go out world beat dancing or do something else that you might not ordinarily do. Bungee jumping, anyone? Then you can break off little pieces of these whole-life experiences, swallow them whole, and bring their freshness back into your work.

Of course, creativity is more than just seeking small pleasures to keep ourselves going. These are places to start, but true creativity is about developing vision that will make things happen on a deeper level. Creativity is about opening up to life and work in such a way that it will precipitate an important change.

When i was writing this book, I woke up one morning out of words. And I remembered how, when I was a child, always reading or writing, my father encouraged me to set aside my pages on occasion and take in the rich universe that was ever beyond my interior world. We would go for long walks and observe ants working in their colonies, the neighbor harvesting grapes in his garden, the moon as it grew from crescent to full.

So on this morning I decided to leave my house for some out-in-nature perspective. I climbed a mountain, sat on a rock, and watched animals at work. Oh, I know that animals don't go to the office as we do, but their days are filled with the work of survival, the job of navigating through their days.

As I watched deer, ground squirrels, soaring eagles, and a mountain lion hunting along a distant ridge, I realized that the difference between animals and humans is that animals don't hunker down, put their noses to the grindstone for eight hours, and then go home and attend to their personal lives. Instead, their days are integrated with everything their existence is about. Their "office" is an entire mountainside, a meadow, a creek, acres of sky, the entire territory where they live and breathe. Their hours are interspersed with hunting, building nests, socializing, grooming, mating, playing, and resting. Their existence is a rhythm of survival and spirit, rest and work—the work of living their lives.

When I returned home to write my chapter, I felt that my outlook had altered quite a lot. I thought, There is much to learn from the ways animals live. I thought, Our workdays would feel more creative if we began to interweave them with the rest of our human experiences. If we opened the windows to our entire world as we performed our work.

Simone Weil said, "Workers need poetry more than bread. They need that their life should be a poem. They need some light from eternity." Perhaps we can experience some of that eternity if we allow ourselves more poetry, more creativity, in our work. If we extend our vision to give us that larger glimpse of the light. If we can create, in the process, a job with a view. On alternate Tuesdays, and a few other days as well.

OVERCOMING WORKER'S
BLOCK

IT'S ONE thing to get more creativity into your work.
To have a job with a view. But what about those projects you can't
seem to get off the ground despite all desperate measures to make
them work? What about those days when you simply don't have
the energy to pull it all together no matter what?

We've all heard of writer's block, the malady that writers
suffer from when the words don't happen. But this phenomenon
doesn't just happen to writers; in fact, it's hit me in all kinds of
jobs. Therefore I prefer to think of it as *worker's* block—
something that anyone can experience when your work isn't
going with the flow.

Worker's block can occur in any type of job: engineering,
psychotherapy, administration, violin making, scientific research
. . . you name it. Probably there isn't anyone who hasn't been
there at some point in his or her career. Whatever term you use,
writer's block, worker's block, the Great Void—a colleague calls
it the Dreaded Brain Fungus Disease—is about creativity or momentum waning. It's about a deep inner voice hollering, "No!" at
the least convenient time. Who knows why? You may have the
most exciting assignment or the most uncomplicated project, but
if you've lost your motivation, you're going nowhere, and you are
stuckstuckstuck.

Galen, a Greek physician who lived in 130 C.E., said that
employment is nature's physician and is essential to human hap-

piness. Things haven't changed in that respect. Our work is still our self-expression, our way of being productive in our lives. We survive through being involved and connected to our world. When we can't move forward as we like, we feel restless, ineffective, and certainly unhappy.

People experience—and deal with—a block in different ways. My sculptor friend Helen feels it as a sort of paralysis and finds that she has no choice but to change directions for a while. But her husband Chris, a French and Italian professor currently writing a book, works it out by plowing through.

When my publisher friend Antoine is blocked, he is overcome by extreme restlessness, what he calls the storm before the calm. When too many projects arrive on his desk at once, invariably with the same deadlines, it drives him "craaaaazy." Since he can't focus on his work in this state, he rechannels his energy by lifting weights or taking a long bike ride. Or, in real emergencies, by running up the steepest mountain trail he knows.

On the other hand, an editor I once knew sometimes worked herself into such mental exhaustion that she couldn't do anything at all. Recognizing her dilemma as a clear case of "burning karma at both ends," she closed her office door, had a good cry, then took a short journey into uninterrupted unconsciousness. When she awoke, she felt refreshed, and the office was filled with her keys-afire typing style once again.

When worker's block happens to me, I feel like my garden in the spring—full of clumps of dirt that have to be broken before flowers can be planted. The thing about clumps is that they are made of potentially good soil. The soil just needs to be turned over and fertilized before seeds can be sown. The same is true with my work. I know that the words are down there somewhere, and if I turn over the clumps of ideas, I'll make some good planting ground. Another thing I do is use a checklist, which gets directly to the point. It breaks up all the clumps.

- *Do something different*. In your work, in your life, in your dreams. The block may be caused by being too close to your daily routine. Try focusing on another project, rearranging your office, or altering your schedule for a day or two. Turn your schedule around in your personal life, too. Take a class or a vacation. Meet a friend you haven't seen for a while for coffee. Do something to fulfill a dream. A complete change of pace can go a long way toward breaking up a block and refreshing your work.

- *Change your perspective.* Helen did this when she found herself in the middle of a large alabaster sculpture and didn't know how to proceed next. She finally decided to trade the large perspective for the small by letting the sculpture sit and carving small whimsical wooden figurines. She discovered that it not only loosened her up, but the figurines turned out to be exactly what she needed to finish the original piece. Later, the figures even turned into a complete series of their own.

- *Work with the mechanics.* A colleague who produces newsletters finds that it helps to work on the mechanical things when he gets stuck. So he repaginates, aligns advertisements, and rechecks his margin spacing. As he explains, dealing with the mechanics maintains a pace while he rebuilds his creative momentum. After the details are in place and the block is over, he can concentrate completely on the creative aspects of the job.

- *Marinate.* Also known as creative procrastination, marination is for those times when your ideas aren't quite seasoned yet. You aren't really blocked, it's just that those ideas need to sit in the vinegar of your subconscious a little longer before the work is ready to be prepared. When I have an article to write, I often sketch out a rough outline, along with a few salient points I want to make. Then I let it all marinate in the back of my head for several weeks. When I finally sit down to work, the piece usually unfolds fairly close to its final version. Novelist John Irving takes marination a step further by considering his characters and plots for four or five years before he actually begins to write. He figures if he is still interested in the book by then, it's a project worth undertaking. And Victor Hugo surely must have been thinking of marination when he said, "A man is not idle because he is absorbed in thought. There is a visible labor and an invisible labor." Marination is the invisible action behind the visible piece.

- *Get physical.* One of my Zen teachers says that when I'm blocked it's because I'm thinking about the project so much that I'm making it too important. This gives it so much power that I am no longer in control. He says, "Go outside and dig the largest hole you can. Don't stop until you are thoroughly exhausted. Then you will be able to work." He's right. I have frequently conquered blocks by digging in my garden or cleaning the house. Many great philosophers, including Aristotle and Nietzsche, developed their famous philosophies while getting physical, in the form of long walks.

- *Find the perfection in imperfection.* A block in your work may be created by an unhelpful perfectionist in your midst—either yourself or a supervisor or an external editor. And perfectionism is one of the best ways I know to sabotage your work. During perfectionistic times, I find it helpful to remember a little Zen wisdom: "Find the perfection in imperfection." Then I scribble ideas at random, begin a project inside-out, and don't worry if it doesn't make sense. I let my project parade about in its underwear until it decides what it wants to be when it grows up and gets dressed.

- *Breathe into the pain.* Several years ago I was Rolfed—a form of deep tissue massage that helps to realign your body and release deep-seated emotions. When my muscles resisted that deep massage, the Rolfer told me to breathe into the pain. The same principle can be applied to work. Maybe this is the last thing you want to do, but I often find that breathing into the pain of a block helps me to let go of my tension and eventually allows me to go more completely into my work.

- *Enlist help.* Talk over your project with a friend or colleague. Another person may be able to offer a new perspective. Or read a few words from a book that gives you inspiration. When I'm blocked my favorites are *Writing Down the Bones* by Natalie Goldberg and *Bird by Bird* by Anne Lamott. The humorous wisdoms in these books always inspire me to renew my momentum, whatever the nature of the task.

- *Go with the flow.* Often worker's block is compounded by pure resistance, which can be alleviated by going with the flow. So if you find yourself pacing, go ahead and pace. If your thoughts take you in circles, follow the swirls. I have often discovered that these seemingly counterproductive motions serve to bring order out of my chaotic thoughts.
- *Enjoy it.* Seriously. Bask in the peace and quiet, the pleasant dullness, the unexpected meditation break. Appreciate the fact that there are no thoughts thrashing about every other second because, realistically, you know that sooner or later they will come crashing down. At which point you will have a heck of a lot of work to do. So give yourself some time off. Take the "calculated waiting" view of the *I Ching*, which suggests nourishing and strengthening yourself in comfort and contentment until the situation turns. Sit back, slowly unwrap a piece of dark peppermint chocolate, and savor every bite.

One last thing. I often talk about putting ideas on my "dream agenda"—writing down problems to be solved before I go to bed, in the event that I come up with answers in my sleep. Skeptical friends laugh at me, but it actually works more often than not. Sometimes a dream takes me to the root of the matter. Other times it even brings a whole new chapter in the middle of the night.

I offer a variety of thoughts for overcoming worker's block because everyone finds a solution through a different process. What works for my friend Helen doesn't work for Chris. A solution for Valerie may be something one of her colleagues wouldn't ever consider. Like anything else in life, you have to find your own rhythm for breaking things up.

And when nothing on the list, even chocolate, does the trick? Well, I have to admit that I worry a little. Okay, maybe I worry a lot. But just before the dragons who are breathing down my neck manage to set the whole building on fire, I go for a walk. During which I assure myself that I am only human, after all, and humans are prone to the occasional block. During which I say out loud that my brain is entitled to a short vacation, even if I am its boss and I would rather it wait until a week from tomorrow. Then, very kindly, I explain to myself that for my holistic health, for the holistic health of the people in my midst, and ultimately for the project at hand, I have to let go. Because even though it *is* my work and it *is* important, and I want it to be a smash success, in most cases if it is a little late, no one—including myself—will *die*.

However you work it through or let it go, worker's block *will* come to an end. Usually in this lifetime, too. But if it doesn't, I take it as a divine sign that it just isn't time for this particular project, in which case I relegate it to the next-life pile and hope someone else gets it the next time around. Meanwhile, I concentrate on my other work. And I keep this list in my desk drawer to marinate. Pass the vinegar, please.

COLEADERSHIP

I KNOW a six-person graphics department at an atmospheric research center that has six directors. That is, the department is governed by a rotating directorship—a coleadership —with each director leading the department two months a year. This "democratic" leadership has been in effect for more than a decade, with few complications.

I was doing contract work in another department at the center when I first encountered this group. Being your basic nonhierarchical sort, I thought this was a wonderful idea: democracy at its finest. Everyone had an equal say in how the business was run. Everyone had an equal level of commitment. The organization encouraged all employees to bring their full selves to the fore— while benefiting from everyone's individual strengths.

The more I considered coleadership, the more I liked it. It was fair and open. It kept everyone involved. It encouraged ongoing communication. It was maybe the best organizational structure to ever hit Workplace Earth, I thought. It was exactly what the employment gods ordered.

As I was about to pronounce coleadership the bee's knees, the cat's pajamas, and the snake's slippers, however, my skeptical side came creeping out and began to slither slowly through my previous logic. It had a lot of out-loud questions. Did each individual *really* have an equal say? Could one voice *actually* be heard as well as the next? If so, would too many voices weaken the system? To which all six members countered with their own question: Who says an effective leadership can't have six strong voices—or even more?

To help me understand, Susan, the longest-tenured member of the group, asked if I had played follow the leader as a child.

"Sure," I replied in my most dubious voice. "Didn't everyone?"

"Okay," she said. "Think back a moment. There were five or six children and everyone took turns at being the leader, right?"

"Weeeell, *mostly*," I agreed, thinking of the bully in my neighborhood, an older boy known as Marty Smarty Pants. Marty's idea of playing follow the leader didn't involve taking turns. It was more like a dictatorship, whereby Marty prevailed upon us to do unpleasant things, like drop big hairy wolf spiders down the front of our shirts and eat squished earthworm pies.

Recalling the taste of earthworm, I wasn't sure that this childhood-game theory was applicable to adult business practices, although I had to admit that the game in my neighborhood eventually evened out. After we overthrew Marty's tyrannical rulership, the rest of us asserted ourselves. We listened to each other's ideas and generally took turns with little dispute.

"See?" Susan said. "This is a similar system, only in the business world. Given the right set of circumstances and the right group of people, it definitely works."

Even my skeptical side had to concede that she had a point. So co-leadership *was* possible. In fact, as Susan explained further, there are several more advantages

- By alternating leader and follower roles, individuals can develop a wider range of skills.
- Each person can enjoy a variety of responsibilities, thus keeping the job fresh.
- The group benefits from a variety of management styles, as well as from changing personalities and personal strengths applied to the management role.

- Both leaders and followers can deepen their understanding of what each role requires, affording everyone greater perspective on the organization as a team. As they step back into the follower role, leaders are reminded of the importance of listening to the rest of the staff.
- If one director is on leave another can easily step in, leaving no gap in the system.
- No one becomes too attached to either a leader or follower role, leaving everyone more open to focus on what Max DePree, author of *Leadership Jazz*, stresses as "ideas, not authority . . . principles, not rules."

As Susan pointed out, these benefits advanced each staff member while reinforcing the team. And, unlike my old nemesis, Marty Smarty Pants, everyone had an opportunity to learn from observing their coleaders manage. Through direct comparison, they easily saw their own strengths, while receiving support for the skills they wanted to build.

I agreed that this made sense. But, I wanted to know, what about conflicts? How could disagreements be resolved without one master voice? Like all decisions, I was told, solutions were reached by consensus. Even if an issue involved only two people, all six leaders would do a "roundtable session" and work it through together. In the event of irreconcilable differences—a situation that occurred only twice in ten years—a manager in the human resources department was on call to mediate.

Obviously, the fact that these six people are personally compatible makes their efforts a success. They share a common philosophy of work and leadership. They agree on the ultimate departmental goals that not only support themselves but serve the overall organization. As long as everyone continues to keep these goals in mind, their coleadership arrangement has the potential to endure for years to come. Because they have the right set of circumstances—and the right group of people—to make it work.

COLEADERSHIP: ANCIENT WISDOM OR FUTURE TREND?

Although leadership by consensus may not be the answer for everyone, I wouldn't be surprised to see more organizations move in this direction, particularly as corporations continue to restructure and "human-sized" companies dominate the workforce. In fact, I have recently come across several more businesses that use coleadership in various forms.

One such organization is a Native American advocacy center where I had a freelance assignment. Here I learned that comanagement is similar to an ancient American Indian tribal tradition that emphasizes one strong leader, or chief, while the others in the community hold equal status. With the exception of the chief, everyone has equal job titles. The philosophy behind this is that each person is viewed as a leader, in the sense that he or she has much to contribute to the benefit of all. In this capacity, everyone supports and enhances one another as they move forward in unison. The result is that hierarchy—and thus competition—is minimized, which the tradition holds as weakening community. On the other hand, a cooperative system increases the overall strength of the group.

Another Native American tradition I witnessed at the center is the talking circle: a meeting where everyone sits in a circle and a staff called a talking stick is passed around. The person holding the stick is the only one who speaks, while the others listen. When that person finishes, he or she passes the stick to the next individual, until everyone has spoken. Through emphasis on open communication—each individual shares ideas and listens attentively—the coleadership strengthens and grows.

Another workplace where I have seen coleadership in action is in the photo department of a large city newspaper. In this situation, staff members learn several jobs, including management positions, and routinely fill in for one another. A photo editor I spoke with says that the daily operations run more smoothly since the department implemented this system.

"It's practical for the department and encourages everyone to become more widely involved rather than remaining in their individual roles," he explained. "Plus, staff members have a greater understanding and appreciation of each other's work. Let's face it, taking on additional job skills increases the chances for professional advancement, and who couldn't use a little of that?" He added, "Part of my job is to talk to other photo editors at newspapers across the country. Role trading is happening everywhere."

This conversation made me consider: Is coleadership ancient wisdom, or is it a future trend? Perhaps a little of both. I still think we will see much more of it, particularly in smaller companies. Because, yes, in some situations it definitely works.

APPLYING COLEADERSHIP IDEAS TO
A TRADITIONAL ORGANIZATION

This is all very well and good, but what if your particular station on Workplace Earth doesn't have coleadership? Can you still benefit from the coleadership philosophy? Can you apply a few of its ideas to a noncoleadership group?

I pondered this for a long time. Deep down, I knew the answer was yes, but I wasn't quite sure how. Then I reread the acceptance speech given by the Dalai Lama when he received the Nobel Peace Prize in 1989:

> Peace starts with each one of us. So much starts within us. When we have inner peace we can be at peace with those around us. When we feel love and kindness for others, it not only makes others feel loved and cared for, but it helps us also to develop inner happiness and peace. Our responsibility is for each other. . . .

"So much starts within us" struck a chord. Peace. Love. Kindness. Yes, these qualities all begin within, and it's good to bring them into the workplace. But what about leadership? Doesn't it start within as well—not just within corporate presidents and tribal chiefs, but in all of us? Don't we as individuals have the responsibility to lead ourselves and, in doing so, lead others by example? Even if we aren't "the leader," can we lead by being a strong and gentle influence, by being mindful in our work and confident in ourselves, by contributing ideas and showing that we want the business to grow?

Coleadership is an interplay of leadership and followership. It's a dynamic give and take, a syncopation of employees' playing off one another's roles. It focuses on the fact that an organization depends upon the union of several strong individuals to make it a success. As the Oriental proverb has it, "Behind an able person there are always other able people." Able people play a variety of roles.

I thought about some of the qualities that make a good leader: understanding . . . effective communication . . . taking genuine satisfaction in the achievements of others . . . learning as much as possible about the business . . . and having a sense of direction, both personally and for the group. These are all qualities that make good followers, too. Qualities that followers can develop in order to apply a coleadership philosophy to a noncoleadership organization.

In considering these qualities, I thought of a few other ways we might manifest more coleadership in our workplaces:

• Take responsibility for our actions . . . in our work performance . . . in our interactions with others . . . in how we contribute to the success of the business.
• Be willing to give the best of our experience and our skills and, when possible, to take the extra step.
• Build constructive, respectful relationships that emphasize honest, open communication and strengthen the work community.

- Recognize the contributions of managers and colleagues and support their efforts.
- Be willing to learn other jobs and fill in as needed.
- Make a point of staying informed about the business on a day-to-day basis, and be certain that we are receiving accurate information rather than making assumptions.
- Be flexible about organizational changes, doing what we can to ease the transitions.
- Watch our leaders closely and absorb their management practices. This will be useful not only in our daily work, but later when we may become leaders ourselves.

Of course, there are many styles of leadership. Whatever the style of our particular workplaces, why not take more personal responsibility? Why not work toward strengthening our organizations (and ourselves) by sharing roles? Why not have six strong voices—or even more?

WORKING MEDITATION

ASIDE FROM quitting your job and moving to a desert island, the best way I know to keep sane at work is to practice meditation. To stop a few times each day, put the workaday chatter on hold, and take a five-minute breather right at your desk—or mountaintop or elevator, or wherever your workplace happens to be. It's a practice that has saved my professional soul for a number of years. I call it Working Meditation.

Valerie and I originally discovered Working Meditation through a collective plan of hyperefficiency. We were both Zen students, we realized how much meditation centered us in our lives, and we thought that more meditation would help us in our work, but our hectic schedules left little extra time. So we decided to bring meditation into the workplace—to meditate as we worked.

As with most plans, this one evolved through trial and error (or trial by fire) before we arrived at just the balanced formula. Plan A involved working and meditating at the same time: taking a deep breath, exhaling, and continuing the slow breathing cycle for nine more breaths as I wrote my current chapter. Sounds efficient, right? It was, except for one small problem. Being an extremely focused person, I have never been very talented at juggling two activities at once (Ringling Brothers or Cirque du Soleil would never hire me, for sure). So when I breathed, I forgot to write. And when I wrote, I forgot to breathe, the result being that I accomplished very little writing, plus the lack of oxygen had me practically turning cerulean, cobalt, indigo, and several other impressive shades of blue.

Concerned that I might spontaneously reincarnate, Valerie felt compelled to take over with plan B. Her idea was to alternate work and meditation instead of doing them simultaneously. She did this by considerably speeding up her work activities to make time for several thirty-minute meditation periods within the day. This worked for a few days, and we thought we were in the home stretch. Unfortunately, it soon caught up with her in the form of serious mistakes like inputting $9,100 on a budget report when she actually meant $1,900. Also, because she was trying to fit more into the day, she was always running late. This wasn't too much of an issue until she ran her car into a ditch one morning in a mad dash to get to work early enough to meditate. As the tow truck pulled her out, Valerie knew that plan B had just bitten the dust.

Shortly thereafter, I attended a retreat where I met an eighty-year-old Zen master named Don Gilbert, an American trained in one of the Korean Zen traditions. In his earlier years, Don had studied Zen while traveling the world as a circus acrobat, so he understood how the juxtaposition of work and meditation could be a delicate balancing act. His suggestion was to incorporate short periods of meditation into our workdays by stopping to sit and breathe for a few minutes several times each day. We didn't need to *go* anywhere to do it; we could meditate right at our desks. Valerie and I breathed sighs of relief. This not only seemed possible—it sounded sane. It was the beginning of what we came to call Working Meditation.

HOW IT WORKS

Working Meditation is based on two concentrations: conscious breathing and the clarification of "mind clutter," what I call the extraneous thoughts that do jumping jacks in my head. Breathing and clearing the mind go hand in hand, as every mental state is reflected in the body and breath. For example, I tend to react to stressful thoughts by holding my breath. My acupuncturist says this creates an energy block in my solar plexus, resulting in considerable tension. Similarly, Valerie has noticed that her breathing becomes shallow when she is angry or apprehensive or when she feels under pressure. Through conscious breathing, it's possible to disperse those messy thoughts, to release that stressful state and find a calmer sense of being in the process. Taking a deep breath is literally like activating your own personal sedative—a sedative that doesn't require a prescription and is abundantly available to you at any time.

I primarily use three Working Meditation exercises. The first is a simple conscious breathing practice. The second involves visualization, which aids relaxation by focusing on a specific image; the one I offer here was inspired by a friend who is a Tibetan Buddhist in the lineage of the Dalai Lama. The third exercise is a variation on walking meditation from the Zen tradition. Depending on my schedule, I work in any one of these exercises, or a combination thereof, every day.

Deskside Breathing Practice (3–5 minutes)

Stop work. Slowly stretch your arms, legs, and neck. Remaining in your chair, straighten your back, position your feet flat on the floor, and rest your hands loosely in your lap. Shoulders should be relaxed, head up. Eyes can be open or closed. Take a deep breath, holding in the air for as long as comfortable. Slowly exhale, so that the exhalation takes longer than the inhalation. As you breathe, note the air moving through your lungs. When thoughts arise, briefly acknowledge them, then let them flow away with the breath. Continue for ten breaths or more. Return slowly to your work.

Variation: Stand or sit in front of a window with a view that you enjoy. Keeping your eyes open, practice breathing deeply while you take in the view. Continue to breathe slowly in and out for five or ten minutes, allowing your thoughts to follow the view.

Ocean Visualization Practice (3–5 minutes)

Close your eyes and take a few deep, slow breaths. In your mind, focus on an ocean. Visualize everything possible about the ocean: its blue-green hue, the smell of sea salt, the way the waves lap rhythmically, shhh, shhh, shhh, against the beige-sand shore. Watch the gulls dip and soar in the ever-changing clouds across the watery miles. Breathe in and out slowly during this visualization, matching your breath to the rhythm of the waves. Continue for ten breaths or more. Return slowly to your work.

Variation: Concentrating on your breath, picture another object such as a rose. Visualize its bright magenta, the velvet texture of its petals, its delicate fragrance, and the nine-spotted ladybug perched on one of its deep green leaves. Imagine yourself carrying the rose to a vase on your desk as you return to work.

This exercise is for a longer break away from your desk, perhaps over the lunch hour:

Zen Walking Meditation Practice (15–30 minutes)

Find a park or a path near your workplace that has no traffic and a minimum of distractions. Place your left hand over your abdomen and your right hand over your left hand, and take a few deep breaths. Now inhale deeply while stepping forward with your right foot. Hold for a few seconds. Now exhale while stepping forward with your left foot. Continue for several minutes, inhaling as you step with your right foot, exhaling as you step with your left foot. As you walk, concentrate only on the activities of breathing and walking, letting go of thoughts as they arise. Slowly end the walk and try to maintain this sense of rhythm and calm throughout the rest of the workday.

I do these exercises between projects or whenever I feel a need to strengthen my concentration and calm my day. Often, I find myself meditating automatically, so the exercises function as natural work breaks. Valerie, on the other hand, has formalized her Working Meditation practice since her mishap in the ditch. Feeling that she needs more structure in her life, she has established a daily ritual that begins with five minutes of breathing at her desk each morning. She does fifteen minutes of walking meditation before lunch and stops for a few minutes of visualization before important meetings. She also uses conscious breathing or visualization at the end of her workday to help transition herself more smoothly into the evening.

MEDITATION AS COMMON SENSE

I heard a talk by Sogyal Rinpoche, author of *The Tibetan Book of Living and Dying*. He said, "Buddha didn't teach Buddhism. He taught common sense." As soon as he said this, I realized that is exactly the way I feel about meditation. Yes, meditation can lead the way to higher consciousness. Yes, it can remind you of how you aren't solitary in your life or your work and are connected to a much larger world. It even has documented health benefits such as lowered blood pressure, decreased heart and respiratory rates, and improved circulation. But when it gets down to the everyday, work-it-out, workaday world, meditation in the workplace keeps me sane. And sanity is pure common sense.

Over the years, Working Meditation has saved me almost daily—both when I'm writing at home and when I'm working in a corporate office. When I practice meditation regularly, it keeps me emotionally centered and better focused. It enhances my creativity and takes me to a deeper place within my work. In business interactions, it increases my understanding of my colleagues and gives me greater perspective in a variety of circumstances—

including the ability to see the lighter side of just about any situation. What else can I say? Meditation at work *works*.

Insight meditation teacher Jack Kornfield says, "Don't let thoughts possess you and don't assume you have to act on them." Regular meditation at work helps me to do both by increasing my awareness of a particular thought . . . encouraging me to step back and view it more objectively . . . teaching me to observe before I react . . . and seeing when a thought should be dealt with and when it should simply fall away. Meditation helps me to drop the thought barriers between myself and my work, and to be more mindful in everything I do. Meditation is, as the samurai say, a way to make your mind your friend.

Valerie and I have found that we can reinforce Working Meditation by doing more formal meditation early in the morning and practicing with our Zen group at least once a week. Attending a week-long retreat once or twice a year is also of enormous benefit, as the centering effects can last for several months.

I have even started sitting groups at work that meet over lunch or during short afternoon breaks. At one of my jobs, I often had six silent people in my tiny cubicle. In the beginning this drew a lot of attention. One colleague thought we were holding an impromptu meeting. Another wondered if we had the scoop on a new company rumor. Someone else was certain that we were plotting to overthrow the administration. What were we really doing? Well, *you* know. Working Meditation.

Of course, you may not think that meditation at work is quite the thing for you. You may have other methods for keeping sane. I received an E-mail from a colleague in Boston, describing an "insane project, with an insane project manager, destined to send us all to white-coat hell." She wrote, "And don't you dare tell me to take a deep breath. What I need is to go into a broom closet and holler 'Shit!' at the top of my lungs."

I meditated on that message for a couple of minutes. I recalled several occasions in my work life that called for a primal scream. Then I E-mailed back, "Go for it. I want to hear that 'Shit!' across the country. But don't forget to breathe."

KEEPING YOUR SANITY

ONE OF the first things I notice when I work in a large corporation is how much collective stress is generated on any given day. It is as if the job god from hell has let himself in through the back door, opened a Pandora's box of heavy workloads, tight deadlines, and potential conflicts in the middle of the office and is running through the building with a megaphone, declaring "Let there be stress!" And, by God, there is.

Add difficult coworkers, even more difficult bosses, restructuring announcements, impending layoffs, and personal agendas to the whole scenario and soon it builds up like the *Calvin and Hobbes* cartoon in which Calvin makes a snowball so large it's impossible to lift, let alone throw. Certainly, he is disappointed that he won't be able to hit his proposed target. Nevertheless, he quickly finds an explanation for the problem: "Reality continues to ruin my life."

This is not to say that large corporations are the only stress generators in the workforce. Of course they aren't. Some days I can feel plenty stressed out just working at home alone. Whatever your situation, work is one of those places where reality can ruin your life on a daily basis if you give it the chance. Considering the variety of unexpected circumstances that arise during the course of a day, the number of opinions trying to reach each single decision and the perpetual workaday noise—including *all that thinking*—well, no wonder. How conceivable is it, in the wake of these elements, that events will stack up exactly the way you want them? How likely that everything will run according to your personal plan? Unless you work in Shangri-la or Utopia or some other professional paradise, not very likely. The fact is that stress can snowball every workday minute. If you aren't on top of it all, your life can feel ruined day after day. So how do you keep from being swayed by everyone and everything you come into contact with during the workday? How do you stay sane when reality keeps getting in the way?

Since my freelance workstyle has brought so many unpredictable situations over the past several years, my workplace sanity has depended upon developing a few strategies to keep the white coats away. Through trial and error, I've discovered that my saving combination is (1) increasing my awareness of what invariably causes stress so I can batten down the emotional hatches when I see it coming; (2) devising some methods of maintaining equilibrium before stress hits; and (3) keeping a few remedies on hand for emergencies. Here are a few thoughts.

THE WORK ENVIRONMENT: PEACEABLE KINGDOM OR NATURAL DISASTER AREA?

I once had to write a newsletter in an office where human volcanoes shouted angrily back and forth, an intercom blasted frequently over my head, and the hallway served as a bowling alley for the company dog. In addition, my project supervisor was a bit dramatic herself—her idea of checking in being to leave thirty "urgent" voice mail messages a day. If nothing was going wrong, she thought it best to blow her top anyway, because it probably would. I have to say that I honestly appreciate direct communication, even expressions of anger when appropriate. I am also a great animal lover—I once rode sixty miles in the backseat of a station wagon with a Shetland pony—and I think natural disasters are fascinating events. However, there is a time and place for everything, and that time and place isn't necessarily at work. In this case, I had to do a million impromptu breathing exercises, invoke the power of my stereo headphones, and chant a mantra of mixed expletives under my breath in order to complete the newsletter on deadline. Although I managed to maintain my sanity, it felt like a major miracle to make it through.

Of course, it's easier to keep sane in offices that are peaceable kingdoms, in workplaces that offer tranquillity and support. Yes, it's more pleasant to have pleasant, even-tempered coworkers, but what about colleagues who operate by volcanic inspiration? What about work environments that are more like natural disaster areas?

Fortunately for me, the merciful employment gods came to my rescue after my newsletter assignment experience by presenting me with their very own best-selling program: *Wisdoms from the Employment Gods: Disaster Control.* Complete with antidisaster music that sounds like water lilies moving across a pond, and confetti, and champagne in a bottle the size of a bottle of white-out to break open at graduation, here are the program's basic steps:

1. Remember that some disasters can be avoided and others will occur no matter what. If a volcano is going to erupt, there isn't much you can do to prevent it. But you might be able to lessen its effects. You can walk away or tap into whatever tends to keep you sane (in my case, music, deep breathing, and working at home or in a remote area of the office). You can appease the volcano demons by apprising them of your project's status on a regular basis—before they are tempted to blow. Then you can ask them, please, pretty please, with organic alfalfa honey on top, to cut back on the voice mail already. A word of warning: If they say no, grabbing your Monte Blanc fountain pen and screaming, "Stop or I'll shoot!" will probably not achieve the desired effects.

2. Step back. Take note in advance of how certain volcano demons and disaster areas affect you. Then put on your hard

hat before they appear. As they creep toward you, try to temper your reactions. Sure, their volcanic selves will be noisy and messy, but can it accomplish anything to spew your own fire back? Is the situation worth four to seven times the risk of disease, which chronically angry or upset people face? Finally, is it really about you, or will your strong reaction just be taking on someone else's problem? Hint: The answers are no, no, and no.

3. Observe that the disaster is happening *around* you, not inside you. Breathe deeply for a few moments and heave a sigh of relief to know that you are a veritable oasis of calm within. Then throw the confetti, guzzle the champagne in one mighty swig, and feel proud that you have successfully activated disaster control. Now retreat into your personal peaceable kingdom, and hunker down to the very important task of doing the work.

HUMOR AND THE ROLLING STONES

Shortly after my graduation from disaster school, Valerie and her boss—she called him Boss Man—arrived at their own disaster plan. This was a great relief, for they had struggled for the longest time to avoid a critical mass. The breach in communication was simple: he saw everything from a corporate five-year-plan perspective, while she tended to think more in the moment. After several screamfests, during which he threatened to fire her or she threatened to walk out, something finally clicked. The result was the following humorous dialogue they agreed to activate during periods of disagreement:

BOSS MAN: I hate Zen people.
VALERIE: I hate business people.
BOSS MAN: I'll get you back in my next life.
VALERIE: No, you won't. I'm more enlightened than you. I'll get you first.

And so forth until they managed to break the ice and get down to the important work of resolving the issue at hand. After which Valerie further broke her own tension by going to her car and playing "You Can't Always Get What You Want" by the Rolling Stones at heart-stopping volume.

Humor and music. Two good ways to get a little sanity into the workplace. If the Rolling Stones isn't your style, any kind of music will do. Mozart: studies show that it actually makes you "smarter" while you are listening. Gamelan: gong/chime orchestral music originally from Asia, composed to encourage spiritual healing. Alvin and the Chipmunks singing "All I Want for Christmas Is My Two Front Teeth." A tape of your sweetie singing "Oh Susanna" in the shower. Your own voice. Whatever works.

I always feel myself lightening up when I hear coworkers laughing down the hall or when someone trills out an aria in the middle of the day. Another plus: singing and laughter are healthful, too. Both have been scientifically proven to relax muscles, stimulate energy circulation throughout the body, increase immune functioning, and stabilize emotions. A good thing to remember next time your colleague hums the Burger King jingle under his breath: instead of being tempted to kill him, maybe you should just sing along.

CREATIVE WORK BREAKS

Some of the sanest professionals I know are the ones who take creative work breaks. They are the ones who step out into the world during the workday for a breath of fresh air, a change of pace, and a taste of something different. The ones who make it a point to create their own oases in the day. For example, I know an environmental engineer who lunches on a rubber raft in the middle of a lake near his office . . . a librarian who plays the organ at a nearby church . . . a computer programmer who drives to the forest and climbs trees . . . and a technical writer who goes to matinees because "trading the small computer screen for the large movie screen gives the work better perspective."

I also know a book publisher who once a week has a lunch-hour massage . . . a hospice nurse who meditates at a Tibetan Buddhist meditation center . . . a photographer who takes a tai chi class in the middle of the afternoon . . . a group of graphic artists who book a corporate conference room and dance the lunch hour away . . . and a social worker who takes her sushi lunch box to the top of a skyscraper and enjoys the view. Meanwhile, there is my veterinarian friend who likes to rendezvous at home with her husband for delicacies of a more private nature. . . .

All of these folks say this creative time away not only rejuvenates their work but gives them greater whole-life fulfillment. Plus, by consciously shifting their focus, they are able to put into perspective the little inanities that lurk throughout the day. Whatever the activity, they also get a refreshing jump-start to a productive afternoon. Why not give yourself a break? Why not enjoy it all?

WALKING

Speaking of creative work breaks, walking is such a simple way to keep sane at work that I almost left it out. I mean, everyone knows about walking, right? It doesn't require fancy equipment. You don't need an advanced degree in exercise science to do it. You don't even need a personal trainer. It's as easy as untangling the vulturesque posture I invariably get into as I sit in front of my computer and heading out the door.

Walking is so basic that we tend to forget about it. And yet it's a veritable lifesaver in terms of stress. It sends nutrients throughout the system, improving respiration and circulation. It increases the body's oxygen levels, which also helps to clear your head. Walking increases endorphin levels, making it one of the most potent stress busters around.

I often remind myself to walk during stressful workdays. It has saved me on oh-so-many I'm-feeling-murderous occasions. Better yet, I try to walk before stress comes knocking at my door. Even better: double the therapeutic effects and walk with a friend.

THE FOOD-MOOD CONNECTION

Although we all have our priorities in terms of food, I am one of those people whose life is greatly affected by what they eat. While an average dose of sugar or caffeine is pleasantly stimulating for my java-guzzling colleagues, the same amount invariably shoots me to the ceiling, through the roof, and into the morning sky. By the time they're enjoying their second cup, I am skyrocketing toward a distant planet. This may sound jolly, maybe even euphoric to some folks, but it is definitely not a state of mind that is conducive to working. Especially when, a few hours later, I come crashing down to earth. Therefore, I stick to one cup of decaffeinated Sumatran in the morning. And remind myself that if I want to keep my workplace sanity intact, food has to be a major consideration.

Herbalist Brigitte Mars, author of several books on plant medicine and formulator of medicinal herbal teas, talks a lot about keeping in balance through food and herbs. First, she advises getting plenty of B vitamins and calcium into your system. This includes eating foods such as oatmeal, yogurt, and tofu; taking B complex and calcium/magnesium supplements; and drinking chamomile tea. B vitamins help calm the nerve centers, enabling a clearer thought process. Calcium, abundant in dairy products and chamomile, is a natural relaxant.

There are also a number of herbs that aid relaxation without having a somnifacient effect. I have found valerian, skullcap, and passionflower to be especially useful for this purpose. They come in capsule and tincture form, so they are convenient to take at work. Essential oils of lavender and rosemary (sniffed from the vial or on a handkerchief) are also calming. These preparations are available at most health food stores.

If you are in need of more energy in the day, you might try "natural high" snacks such as apples, pears, sunflower and pumpkin seeds, and almonds. These foods are also high in antioxidants, which are important to boosting the immune function and warding off disease. Peeling an orange or grapefruit in the middle of the day has an energizing effect, as does drinking a simple cup of peppermint tea.

You might also supplement with energy-boosting herbs, among them ginseng, astragalus, ginkgo, and St. John's wort. I know many people who benefit from these herbs at work, including several who have radically improved their concentration and memory through the regular use of ginkgo, which has been scientifically proven to improve brain function. Similarly, studies show that St. John's wort consistently elevates spirits and eliminates depression.

Because I have a naturally caffeinated personality, I don't often use energizing herbs. I mostly stick with B vitamin supplements and chamomile tea, and I eat a lot of fruits, vegetables, and seeds throughout the day. But moderation in everything including moderation, I always say. Chocolate, anyone?

Of course, once you get a handle on professional pandemonium, things may not be quite as exciting as they used to be. In fact, you may find the ensuing serenity a bit unnerving, even—gulp—boring. Are you sure you're ready to give it all up? Maybe not. I actually know quite a few professionals who wouldn't trade in their hectic schedules for the world. These are the folks who strive for stress, clamber for chaos, and dash for the most deadly deadlines. As one of my Type A writer friends elaborates, "My whole life is based on stress. What would I do without it? It moves me and shakes me, shapes me and makes me. It stirs up my creativity. It reminds me that I am *alive*."

Whatever works, I say. If you're a confirmed Type A, don't let my sanity techniques get in the way. In case you don't belong to that club, however, I hope some of these ideas help. But remember, the key to keeping your sanity is to go beyond just coping. Find out not only what works, but what *keeps working* over and over again.

ALTERNATIVE WORKSTYLES

RECENTLY, OUTSIDE a local "laundri-mutt," a woman presented me with her business card:

RAMONA K——	• *Piano Lessons*
PROFESSIONAL SERVICES	• *Dog Walking*
444-CARE	• *Cat Care*
	• *House-sitting*
	• *Expert Plant Care*
20 Years Experience	*References/Bonded*

Disappointed in hearing that I didn't have a dog and that dog washing was merely a spectator sport for me on my way to a nearby café to meet a friend, we nevertheless struck up a conversation—her motivation being that I was a potential client with possible contacts, mine being that yes, I do occasionally require pet sitting. Also, I was intrigued by her particular combination of services and wanted to know more.

"Have you really been working like this for twenty years?" was the first thing I wanted to know.

"Oh, yes," she replied, "and then some."

"Full time?"

"Well, mostly," she said. "Some times are busier than others. I generally have more work in the summers when people take their vacations. Then there are a few dogs that I walk year round over lunch hour, and I have customers who travel on weekends. And some of my piano students have been around for years."

"How did you get into this particular combination of jobs?"

She shrugged. "Just fell into them. Had a few things I enjoyed, so I started doing them. Somehow it all worked out."

"How do you get your work? Do you advertise?"

Ramona gave me a *look*. "Have you seen advertising rates lately?"

I nodded knowingly. I didn't advertise either.

"I *am* in the phone book, and I get a few customers that way," she said. "But mostly I find my clients through word of mouth and by posting cards on bulletin boards at grocery stores, veterinarians, and such. And by meeting people around town like you."

At this point we both smiled and Ramona looked at her watch. "You done interviewing me now?" she said. "I have an appointment with a Mr. Rottweiler across town, and he gets a mite growlish when I get there after his dinnertime."

"Hold on to my card, now," she continued, pulling a few fine gray hairs off my sleeve as a parting gesture. "And here, take another. Just in case. I'm not psychic or anything, but I'd be willing to bet you have a cat, maybe two."

She grinned, as she caught my nod. "If those cats need piano lessons next time you go on vacation, give me a call."

PATCHWORKING

They say that truth is stranger than fiction, and employment is no exception. You never know what you will find, or where you will find it, never mind whose professional path you will cross.

It used to be that Ramona's workstyle—what I call patchworking—was considered an oddity, practiced mostly by gypsies, eccentrics, and people in the arts who supplemented their creative incomes. You simply didn't know a lot of folks who worked this way. Now, as a larger number of people seek alternatives to the traditional career track, patchworkers like Ramona are more prevalent.

I meet quite a few professionals who are trading in their nine-to-fives for a crazy quilt of part-time jobs. Among them are an ex–corporate lawyer who combines basic legal services with stockbrokering and technical editing; a building appraiser who teaches archaeology classes at a community college; a psychother-apist who also has an astrology practice and writes travel features for airline magazines; a choreographer who runs an Alexander Technique institute and teaches yoga; a young mother who does freelance research projects as well as teaching Taoist movement classes and meditation for women; and a hairdresser who does freelance hair photography and sells herbal supplements.

As with Ramona, there are a number of reasons people are attracted to this particular workstyle:

- To be able to do *all* of the work they enjoy rather than being limited to—and maybe burning out on—a single field.
- To combine the skills and talents that, individually, they might be pressed to make a full-time living at.
- To have a flexible schedule.
- To keep their work lives interesting and varied.
- To be able to work at home.
- To have more time for themselves.
- Last but not least, to be *their own boss.*

Others have their own special reasons for patchworking. Nell, an electrical engineer, is a university professor on Tuesdays and Thursdays and spends the rest of her week selling real estate. She is drawn to this job for the yin-yang factor. "Engineering is very masculine," she explains, "whereas real estate draws more feminine energy because there are more women than men who look at houses. It's a wonderful balance."

How did these patchworkers get started? Everyone I talk to admits that it didn't happen overnight. As is the general rule for beginning home-based businesses, no one simply quit their "day jobs" and ventured cold turkey into their new workstyle. Rather, they established each patchwork profession as a moonlighting project or from a previous business contact. Then they eased into their business by gradually backing off on the hours of their regular jobs, like the lawyer spending less time on legal services and more time on technical editing. And the building appraiser reducing his appraisal hours while taking on more and more archaeology classes. And the hairdresser giving more of his clients to his colleagues as he built his photography portfolio and supplement business.

Generally, they all admit (and I have experienced this myself) they have to plan on working fairly hard in the beginning until their client base is established and their cash flow is in order. After that, they get used to piecing it all together. They are able to settle into a routine.

SEASONAL EMPLOYMENT

Another form of patchworking is seasonal employment. Common among recreation professionals, these jobs are held by people who teach skiing or lead snowshoe treks in the winter and instruct kayaking, climbing, or swimming during the summer. Whatever the sports combination, recreation patchworkers are avid outdoorsfolks who live for the seasons. As my good skier/rafter friend Elsa says, "What could be better than being on the move and getting paid at the same time?"

Seasonal positions are also attractive to students and teachers seeking supplemental income when school is out of session and to retirees who sporadically pick up extra cash. Such opportunities abound in the summer; they include stints through guest ranches, garden centers, recreation areas, resorts, sports arenas, retail shops geared toward summer sales, house-painting companies, pet-sitting businesses, construction and street maintenance crews, and corporate office work (substituting for employees who are on vacation).

Winter possibilities are less plentiful, although there are numerous holiday retail positions (including UPS and other delivery services), as well as ski resort opportunities. One season I puppeteered in a toy store at Christmas. Another season I cashiered at a university bookstore for the January beginning of semester rush. I have also done seasonal floral design work for Valentine's Day, Easter, Mother's Day, Thanksgiving, and Christmas.

Many catalog mail order houses hire seasonal customer service employees. Some of the granddaddies of these businesses are beginning to cooperate with each other to "share" order takers. Through this system, workers move through catalog sales seasons, taking cheese orders at one company in the fall, shifting to a popular clothing retailer for Christmas, then to another mail order business for the months of gardening and summer recreation, and so on. This system benefits workers by offering them full-time employment (the companies are also getting together to offer benefits), while the businesses retain valuable employees—a win-win situation for all.

INTERNSHIPS

Among the seasonal opportunities are summer internships, which are increasingly available in a variety of professions. It used to be that these short programs were geared toward college students as part of their training, or as a bridge between receiving a degree and becoming full-time professionals, as with physicians, veterinarians, and the like. But now many internships are open to anyone, regardless of profession or age, and continue for a year or more. I know a number of thirty-, forty-, and even fifty-something interns who work as newspaper photographers, computer programmers, and public relations writers, to mention a few. One man I recently heard about walked into his college career office with no clue about what he wanted to do and walked out with an internship at Bill Moyers's production company. He has since produced shows for ABC and National Geographic and is currently a field producer for a group that produces documentaries.

All of these folks are finding intern positions to be important opportunities for gathering job-related experience and making job contacts in their fields. How did they get into their programs? Some checked university career centers. Others called businesses directly and asked what internships were available and how they could apply. I've also known professionals who have made the leap from temporary positions into internship programs at their assigned businesses.

CONTRACT WORK

"How does Santa get to all the houses in one night?" I overheard a young child ask his father one Christmas.

"I think he probably contracts it out," replied the dad.

This exchange took place shortly after my book, *Temp*, was published, and I couldn't help laughing out loud. Having worked for several companies myself and seeing a growing segment of the workforce move toward contract work, I could well believe that Santa had finally jumped on the bandwagon himself.

Contracting is another alternative workstyle that more people are turning to, in the form of independent contracting, freelancing, or taking assignments through staffing services. Just about every field uses contract professionals, including medical and legal services, engineering firms, all areas of accounting, and technical writing. A research and development firm where I sometimes freelance has several engineers who operate on a contract basis. The last person who cleaned my teeth was working through a medical staffing service to cover for the regular hygienist, who was on maternity leave. Even one of my veterinarians is a contractor filling in as the full-time veterinarians take vacations. And, of course, every year, at every shopping mall, there is a contractor in a red suit posing as Santa.

While many contractors hope to find more long-term employment, others see many advantages to working on a short-term basis. Some use contract assignments to maintain cash flow between jobs. Many enjoy the exposure to a diverse number of companies. Some like the flexibility that this workstyle has to offer. Some find that a routine job may turn into something *very* interesting—like my friend Ames, who made the leap from temporary administrative assistant to corporate publication designer at a national coffee distributor. Others find unexpected benefits—like my cousin Mark, who met his wife on a short-term assignment.

A few contractors thrive on the temporary factor. A Zen-type computer programmer I know calls himself a "catch-and-release employee." He says, "When you realize the only permanence truly is impermanence, you don't get so caught up in the organization or the politics, and you have a little distance from your employer. You can just focus on the work. And you tend to keep your options open. "

Any alternative workstyle involves being open to the options, which can appear at any moment. Often those options are even within you. I gained a stronger sense of my own mobility when I went freelance with my work. I more readily saw the myriad possibilities. I saw how many skills I could learn on any given project and how I could transfer these skills from job to job. Most importantly, working alternatively taught me to view livelihood as relying more on myself. It taught me to see that instead of expecting one employer to provide for me, I can count on my own efforts to keep myself employed. This revelation is like waking up. And within that awakening lies true personal freedom, a sense of inner security that *no* employer can provide.

Is Money a Dream?

In the dream, I was in the checkout at the Ideal Market, watching other people's groceries ride down the conveyor belt like rush-hour traffic. The line was long, and I stared at the bright splashes of red, green, purple, and orange traveling by. Finally it was my turn. As my assortment of vegetables headed down the ramp, I reached for my wallet and pulled out three five-dollar bills. As I started to hand them to the cashier, however, I realized that they were sassafras leaves. I lifted them to my nostrils and all activity fell away. I was completely immersed in the sassafras, suspended in time. . . .

I had this dream several years ago, right after the publication of my first book—ironically, a guidebook to botanicals. I had recently made the transition to freelance writing after ten years of full-time positions, and although I had money in my wallet, not sassafras, my income *was* much less than I had previously been accustomed to.

At the same time, I was doing some of my most creative work ever, with more motivation than I ever knew possible. I had the flexibility in my work I had always craved. I had ample time for the nonwork activities most important to me—relationships, Zen, the arts, travel, volunteering. And instead of commuting home at rush hour and dashing into the Ideal Market along the way, I was able to shop during less frenetic periods of the day.

That year, I began taking long walks on the mountain trails beyond my house in the late afternoons, and suddenly the world seemed a larger and brighter place. I'm not sure if this was because my work was going well . . . I had more time for meaningful activities . . . my spiritual practice was deepening . . . or a combination of these. But I clearly remember that all the sights, sounds, and smells of the natural world came alive at that time. I noticed everything from the changing shape of a stratocumulus cloud to a praying mantis walking along the trail to the fleeting aroma of the sassafras tree as I brushed a lower branch. It was as though all my senses were on fire, in particular, smell—a sense I had paid little attention to in the past. This made me realize my dream was making a pun on my newfound lifestyle: I had shifted my focus from *cents* to *scents*.

Though we can all agree that aromatics are pleasant, both in dreams and in reality, obviously we could never live on scents alone. Let's face it, life is expensive. We may be able to pay for food with scents in our dreams, but in real life we need cents to survive, not to mention quite a few dollars. And, whether by the traditional nine-to-five workstyle or an alternative, the majority of us have to eke out some kind of living in exchange. Ideally, this livelihood supports us in our efforts to have quality lives. Ideally, it has a sufficient salary to support our basic needs as well as increase our savings and investments.

The more I thought about my dream, the more I realized its basic message: Pursue a freelance workstyle, enjoy your work, enjoy your life; at the same time, pay attention to the necessary financial adjustments. Don't just make it work; make it a success.

FINANCIAL KARMA VERSUS FINANCIAL ENGINEERING

I have a friend who doesn't believe in money. To him, it's a fairy tale handed down by a capitalist society, a mere abstraction. In his mind, money has no basis in reality, dollar signs are mere symbols, money is an ethereal dream.

Indeed, this friend does seem to be one of those people for whom money simply appears. He lives on credit, has no savings, and buys whatever he pleases when he has the whim. And always, *always*—when he comes up short, there is an unexpected inheritance from long-lost Uncle Aloysius or a "little gift" from Cousin Elsinore. I can't believe it; it's really quite amazing.

As a mutual friend observes, this man obviously has extraordinary financial karma. Also, she points out that his Jupiter—known as the great beneficent planet—is in the eighth house of his astrological chart. This is the house of other people's money, and Jupiter hanging there indicates additional income from inheritances, insurance policies, and other assorted, maybe even unexpected, gifts. Not a bad place for beneficence to be.

Of course, when yours truly heard this, she scrambled to her own chart to see where Jupiter lived (you are probably doing the same even as we speak). "Holy Toadscales!" quoth she (an oath she once saw scribbled on a New York subway wall), upon seeing that Jupiter was definitely not in the eighth. "No inheritances. No insurance policies. No Uncle Aloysius or Cousin Elsinore. Oh, well. I guess my financial karma this lifetime is about earning my own way."

Dale Carnegie, the author of self-help books such as *How to Win Friends and Influence People*, said, "About 15 percent of one's financial success is due to one's technical knowledge and 85 percent is due to skill in human engineering." I read this shortly after I went freelance, around the same time I had the sassafras dream. I thought, Yes, that is the answer. Since I needed to rearrange my finances in order to make my new workstyle succeed, and good financial karma and beneficence were obviously out of the question, I had to activate my skills to make it work. I decided to become a financial engineer.

My first step in the engineering process was to write down my priorities. Of course, I already knew what they were, but seeing them on paper made it all seem more tangible. Confronted by the words in black and white, I had a better sense of what I had to work with and what I had to work toward. The more I read them, the more I realized that the financial requirements of my priorities were low. This would make my new workstyle not only possible but probable. Even so, as I wouldn't have the predictable income of a full-time job, I would be operating somewhat on what I called "maybe money," meaning it would still be necessary to make some adjustments, both emotional and financial, to manage the change.

In order to work with this change, I decided to conduct an interview with myself to get a better sense of my direction. I began by considering the following questions:

- Can you live and work the way you want—on a smaller income?
- How much do you *really* need—for now and for the future?
- What are your largest financial requirements—mortgage, food, health maintenance, daily living expenses? Will they be sufficiently met on a freelance income?
- Will you be lessening some of your requirements by working at home—less driving, fewer business clothes, eating at home more instead of out?
- How can you make the best use of a modest income by investing small amounts of money . . . by finding higher-interest savings plans . . . by targeting areas for cutting back?
- Can you reduce expenditures by going easy on or eliminating credit card purchases . . . by taking advantage of sales, bulk food rates, discount services, and secondhand items . . . by going out to dinner only once a week instead of twice?
- Can you learn to be less of a consumer, to live simply and with less "stuff"?

Beginning with "less stuff," I saw obvious areas to work with, including my day-to-day expenses. Like buying pasta and lentils in bulk instead of the more expensive packaged leading brand. And considering where secondhand items would work as well as new. I even took a look at my hair and wondered if I could simplify my hairstyle by having it trimmed at a "cost-cutter's" shop instead of a high-end salon. Next I sent my checkbook to Weight Watchers while I stayed home, counted my pennies, and looked at where I could reduce my budget even more.

At first, cutting back required a certain amount of discipline, but I soon saw it was easier than I had originally thought, especially as I found myself getting excited over bargains and being proud of myself for resisting a dress or household gadget that a year before would have been to die for. I came up with little tricks such as seeing how many days I could go without spending money, and walking around a store carrying an item I fancied until I felt like I already owned it and the urge was gone.

Meanwhile, I got into a cleaning-house mentality. Sold books I no longer needed to used bookstores. Sent unused clothing to a consignment shop or Goodwill. Held a garage sale to get rid of other unwanted household items. It all felt symbolic: getting rid of the old and beginning anew. And I was surprised at how quickly little savings accumulated from such simple efforts. True, it was a crazy penny-ante savings plan, but it seriously added up.

It was around this time that I had a major fireworks-type revelation: there was a difference between the money I *thought* I needed and what I realistically required. I could set aside funds, make a few investments, have the things I truly needed such as wholesome food and good health care. I could still practice generosity by budgeting for charitable donations. Yes, I could live a fulfilling life with my freelance workstyle. I could even have a few occasional luxuries, too.

I couldn't believe it. Maybe I didn't have good financial karma like my friend, but I did have a knack for financial engineering. And financial engineering *worked*.

I soon found that I wasn't alone. Shortly after I entered my own simplification program, I received a letter from a woman named Dana who had recently made similar lifestyle and workstyle transitions. In Dana's case, she engineered herself out of a

$50,000-plus financial services officer position in Texas that no longer fulfilled her and into a job with less stress that she enjoyed more, in Washington state.

She wrote, "It was the high pay, high stress, we need you here twelve hours a day type job that I decided was no longer a good fit for me after eight years. It took two years remaining in that job to pay off all of the debts I had accumulated trying to make up for the fact that I wasn't happy with my situation. However, I eventually did it. That gave me great courage in realizing I *can* do whatever I want and my job does not define me. When I left, so many associates said they wished they could afford to do the same thing. I told them, 'You can, you just have to focus and put your mind to it.' "

When Dana decided to leave financial services, she put herself on the serious debt-clearing program outlined in *Your Money or Your Life: Transforming Your Relationship with Money and Achieving Financial Independence* by Joe Dominguez and Vicki Robin—a book that has assisted in my own transitions. Dana followed the steps for examining her relationship with money, replacing her financial cravings with more personal fulfillment, and gaining more financial control over her life. She learned how, as Dominguez and Robin termed it, "to start making a living instead of a dying."

With her debts finally paid, Dana moved from Texas to Seattle, worked part time in a vegetarian restaurant, and took temporary assignments while she searched for a new direction. Within a year, one of the assignments turned into an offer she couldn't refuse. "It doesn't pay as much as I'm used to," she wrote, "but the work is so much more enjoyable and now that I know how to live on less, I can focus more on the other priorities in my life."

VOLUNTARY SIMPLICITY

I didn't know this in the beginning, but when Dana and I made our lifestyle changes, we were embarking on a lifestyle called vol-

untary simplicity. At the time, I didn't have a name for what I was
doing. Nor was I trying to follow a particular trend or political
movement. I genuinely wanted to add more meaning and creativity to my life and my work, and simple living seemed like the best
solution. It wasn't until later that I realized I was on the cutting
edge of a new movement, that I was participating in a lifestyle
practiced by thousands of people across the country—a lifestyle
that focuses on a higher quality of life based on less. Since I'm
your basic nongroupie, it's a good thing I didn't know I was participating in a movement or I might have run the other way.

Currently one of the top ten trends listed by the National
Trends Institute, voluntary simplicity is about striving toward a
life that Duane Elgin, author of *Voluntary Simplicity*, describes as
"outwardly simple, inwardly rich." Voluntary simplicity is about
living more fully, more spiritually, being more conscious of the
value of our lives and interrelationships. It is about placing less
value on money and objects and more on a higher quality of life.

It's been more than a decade now since I began living this
lifestyle. And even though I no longer focus completely on a freelance workstyle, simplicity feels more natural, more right with
every year. Most importantly, I feel more creative, more spiritual,
more giving in relationship and community, more fortunate to be
alive, even though I live on less. In fact, most days I feel incredibly
wealthy in oh-so-many ways.

Chögyam Trungpa, the Tibetan spiritual leader, said, "There
is a great deal of misunderstanding about wealth. Generally being
wealthy means that you have lots of money, but the real meaning
of wealth is knowing how to create a goldlike situation in your
life. That is to say, you may have only twenty dollars in your bank
account, but you can still manifest richness in your world."

I'm not advocating that people quit their jobs, shrink their
checkbooks to twenty dollars, and sit around all day smelling the
sassafras. Of course, money isn't a dream. But it is possible to
achieve your dream workstyle if you're willing to work with it.
We all have the potential for creating a goldlike situation, whatever our workstyle may be.

Getting
Out

The Job from Hell

Okay, this is it: the moment of truth. To quit or not to quit: that is the question. To stay or not to stay.

To stay is to prolong security . . . to quit is to ignore that small but powerful abstraction called money. To stay is to invite stress . . . to quit is to have no alternative plan. To stay is to have familiar surroundings . . . to quit is to launch into the unknown. To stay is to give in . . . but to quit is to give up, and you aren't the type to quit without a fight.

Still, you've only been at work for an hour and you are already at the end of your professional rope. You've had it up to the rooftop of the Empire State Building, to the highest tip of the highest spike of the Statue of Liberty. And speaking of liberty, you don't know if you can afford the time to read this whole chapter because you are that close to liberating yourself from the situation. Desperation has never been this desperate. You are on the verge of walking away from the Job from Hell.

To quit or not to quit: what will you do?

Quick, sit down. Take three deep breaths. Now consider a few triage strategies that have saved my own ragged soul.

1. Go home sick. Immediately. Don't offer a lengthy explanation, just say you aren't feeling well. If you are that upset, you're probably green enough about the gills to ward off any suspicion. Stay home for a day or two and think about all the reasons that it is the Job from Hell. Are these reasons justification

for quitting, or is there something you can do? Make a list of possible solutions. Consider a variety of alternatives. Meanwhile, be kind to yourself. Take a nap. Read. Buy some flowers. Get a massage. Watch an escapist movie. Do whatever it takes to recharge your energy enough to initiate a serious change.

2. Instead of taking sick leave, work at home for the rest of the day. Or work in a remote area of your building where you can be alone. Over lunch, update your résumé. Browse through the classifieds and check the job postings on the Internet. See what else is out there before you call it quits.

3. Take a break with a sympathetic friend or colleague. A good listener can be a godsend on such occasions. This person may be able to offer valuable objectivity about your situation, as well as make a few helpful suggestions.

4. Take a notebook to a place away from your office and write out the problem. Several of my colleagues report that this is their first line of defense in an emotional emergency since the problem becomes clearer through the writing process and can later be reread. In fact, studies show that the act of writing can actually decrease stress levels in the body.

Get your feelings down to the basics. Determine if it is truly and completely the Job from Hell or if it is simply one element of the job that makes the whole situation seem hellacious. A friend of mine realized through writing that the issue wasn't her actual job as much as it was one challenging individual in her department. Once she saw this in black and white, she decided to voice her concerns. Though she and her coworker weren't the best of friends ever after, they did agree to disagree and to allow each other a wider berth.

If you are a writer—and even if you aren't—you can take the writing process one step further and turn a bad situation into a good story. One of my colleagues regularly creates humorous fiction pieces from her negative work experiences. By the time she finishes exaggerating the details and characters, she's had a few stress-relieving laughs, plus she has a fiction piece that she publishes in a literary magazine.

5. Go for a long, brisk walk. Ask yourself if your dissatisfaction is less about the job and more about another area of your life that is unfulfilled. When Valerie did this, she discovered that the real problem was in her marriage. She eventually solved the problem by getting a divorce instead of quitting her job.

6. Take a vacation. This might be the perfect time to get away. Maybe far, far away. My friend Louis flew to Greece for two weeks during one job crisis. While he was gone he calculated how much he had in savings, set a goal to find another job within six months and—bonus of all bonuses—he met the love of his life on the Grecian beach. He later quit his job *and* got married.

7. Give yourself permission to quit on the spot. *But don't do it.* Instead, imagine yourself saying the words, walking out the door and enjoying sweet liberty all the way home. Envision yourself in a new job, a new city, a new life . . . maybe even in Greece. Sometimes just reminding yourself that you are free to leave relieves the pressure. You can work on a few answers later when you feel more calm. Meanwhile, unless you are independently wealthy, hang on to that job until you have another source of income to back it up.

Naturally, whether to stay or leave depends on the situation, the severity of the circumstances, how long you've been juggling these particular feelings, and your level of tolerance. It also depends on whether there is an actual possibility for real change or if you've clearly exhausted your options. What do you have the power to solve? What is out of your control? Can you remain in the situation and still keep heart and soul together, or is the only real solution to move on?

I have entertained these questions many times during Jobs from Hell. To quit or not to quit. To stay or not to stay. The overwhelming temptation is always to walk out the door and work out the details later. The drawback here is that, in looking back, I would sometimes wonder if there was one more thing I could have done. And if it was wise to give up that income source at that particular moment. I would also wonder about the residual fallout—that is, if I might face similar circumstances (or worse) the next job around.

So mostly—unless the situation seriously jeopardizes my mental or physical health—I tend to choose two simultaneous solutions. Check out other options, aggressively if necessary. Meanwhile, work it out.

TO STAY

You probably can't believe I titled a chapter "The Job from Hell" and then offer encouragement to stay. I know it sounds goofy, but there are jobs from hell and then there are Jobs from *Hell*, if you know what I mean. The latter are threatening situations that are beyond repair. They are the jobs where you bail out fast. They are crises that require emergency care, usually in the form of an extended leave of absence or immediate resignation. I talk more about these jobs in the second half of this chapter.

The other jobs from hell are little devils that give you a good workout. They present situations that keep you in mental shape because they force you always to come out of yourself. They push you to interface directly with your environment. These jobs are good teachers that prompt you to communicate, to solve problems, to prioritize, and to grow out of your limitations. Sure, they are the kind of teachers you also give nasty names to, but you later come to appreciate them because they confer little wisdoms that occur with experience.

In astrology, they say that nothing happens in your life until you are ready for it. I *hate* that. I mean, who says I'm ready for the boss from hell? And who says I'm actually prepared to take on a job that makes me feel uncomfortable, but somehow I can learn to turn it around? Nonetheless, I have to admit that I do manage to come up with the resources to deal with the situation, so when I see myself walking on a tightrope decision of "to quit or not to quit," I activate my industrial-strength nerves and try to find my balance. Even if it does stress me out to the very end of my rope. Even if it makes me cry or makes me mad. Actually, sometimes a little open anger can be a healthy thing, as it clears out the pent-up emotions that keep us from being productive and opens the channels to better communication. If you think about it, anger can be very spiritual, too, because it strips away the extraneous and gets you right down to the basics. It opens you up to a clearer way of thinking.

An architect I once worked with felt the same way. Several times, I saw her get down to the basics by throwing her slide rule to the floor, screaming a single expletive, and taking a short nap on her work table. Yes, I know this sounds like a tiny tantrum—it was. It was also a great way for her to relieve stress, the Gestalt approach to sudden deadline pressure. And it worked. After she awoke, she felt much better, and she was able to meet the deadline without a hitch.

Sometimes when you look jobs from hell directly in the eye, you can see good advice in ancient proverbs like "Trouble brings experience and experience brings wisdom" and "The best way out of a difficult situation is through it." Then you start to seek answers such as talking over a communication problem with a difficult colleague, speaking with a project leader about alleviating a deadline situation, or asking to transfer to a more challenging project. I've noticed that when I go directly into a problem, my colleagues respect me for my openness and are usually willing to make more changes that I anticipated.

Valerie, who used to do temporary accounting work and probably has encountered more jobs from hell than most of us, says that sometimes going directly into it is about facing yourself. What she means is that sometimes she contributes to her own job from hell by making it so. That is, when she makes a statement like, "This is the job from hell," she ends up feeling stuck with it. Which somehow gives the job more strength. It firmly reminds her that *it* is in charge until the scenario becomes an all-out siege, with her saying, "I *have* the job from hell," and the job countering, "You want hellacious? Well, I'll *give* you hellacious!" And it escalates from there.

On the other hand, if she decides to withdraw from the battle, the job from hell backs off, too. Its power begins to wane. Maybe this is because she is spending less time thinking about her dislikes and more time focusing on the actual work and getting to know her colleagues. Maybe it's because, at this point, she begins to recall that even some of her favorite work situations sometimes felt like jobs from hell—jobs that, with some creative thinking, she was able to turn around.

TO QUIT

Having said all of the above about working things out, I will now say that sometimes the best answer is to quit. Because, as my yoga-teacher friends say, a good workout is meant to be only that: it isn't supposed to kill you. Sometimes, no matter what you do, you just have to accept the fact that you aren't compatible with the company, that you and your boss will never see eye to eye, that your colleagues are from another planet, and there isn't a popsicle's chance in hell that the situation is going to give you a smidgen of what you want. In short, it truly is the Job from Hell. Time to get the hell out.

But how do you know when enough is enough? How do you gauge when you've exhausted every possibility? Chances are that you will just *know*.

Everyone has a different sign. I know it's time when I have recurring nightmares—usually having to do with my car crashing into a brick wall—a message that I'm not getting the idea on a conscious level so my unconscious is taking charge. My colleague

Annie, another freelance writer, breaks out in hives—enormous red splotches that invariably go away when *she* goes away from the situation. And Valerie, who has the most creative unconscious I have ever known, craves shark when she is at the end of her employment rope, which she swears never happens at any other time. Her reasoning is based on cause and effect. As she explains it, she doesn't usually eat shark because she likes to swim in the ocean. If she eats shark, then maybe a shark will come along and think it's okay to eat *her.* Therefore, she says, when this craving appears, she knows her intuition is telling her to bail out because she's asking to be eaten alive.

Sometimes the job from hell isn't so obvious. Especially if the business is spiritually based or offers other obvious benefits to the community. This was what happened with Zach, who once worked in a store that sold vitamins, herbs, and spiritual publications. "At first I thought I was doing a great service, selling products that promote physical well-being and spiritual growth," he told me. "Then I discovered that the owner wasn't giving service to her own employees. You never knew from day to day if she would be Dr. Jekyll or Mr. Hyde, we didn't get breaks, even on an eight-hour shift, and she frequently docked people's pay for reasons that made sense to no one but her. When I asked my boss if she knew some of these practices were illegal, she replied that I should feel fortunate to work for a business that was dedicated to the well-being of humanity. I guess that was supposed to justify her behavior, but I couldn't see it. I had to get out."

Every job should be a place of nourishment for everyone involved. A situation where everyone feels he or she is giving and receiving to the mutual benefit of employer and employee. A situation where people treat each other—and themselves—with kindness and proper respect. Because employment is about give and take, mentally as well as financially. When this isn't the case, it degenerates into dis-ease and maybe even serious disease, as one of my colleagues discovered when she ended up in the emergency room with stress-induced arrhythmia. Indeed, research reports that many heart attacks occur on Monday mornings; for some folks, facing another work week is just too much to ask.

No job is worth jeopardizing your mental and physical health, not to mention the ill effects of job-related stress on personal relationships and the rest of your life. If a company's motivation feels wrong, or your boss is unusually difficult, or the situation poses a threat to your mental or physical well-being, it's time to bail out.

Try not to burn a bridge in the process—especially when you're standing on it, as a friend of mine likes to say. You never know when you may want to cross a particular bridge again. But don't worry too much if you do. I have burned bridges right to the ground, only to discover that I could be like the phoenix and create new opportunities with the ashes. I have rechanneled the hot ashes of my anger into finding more solid passageways in a better direction. I have composted the ashes into lessons that could be applied to subsequent jobs. Once or twice, I have even discovered that a bridge can be rebuilt, such as the time I was fired in a political struggle and the company later became one of my most lucrative freelance accounts. Still, it's better to keep your bridges intact if you can. At the same time, give serious thought to your options and consider the following:

- Find out if you are eligible for a stress-related disability leave. I worked with a woman who qualified for disability through a note from her dentist. Apparently, her job was affecting her so badly that she was injuring her mouth by grinding her teeth.
- Consider an unpaid leave of absence, which would buy you time to job hunt while maintaining company-paid benefits— and, if necessary, an option to return to your current position.
- Seriously weigh the situation. If it's caused by emotional abuse or sexual harassment or a hazardous work environment, find out your legal rights. Not only might you have a case, but a leave of absence could be covered by your employer under a

special clause. It might even be grounds for unemployment benefits.

- Find out if your insurance covers counseling. Many plans will pay for up to ten sessions of therapy or even more. A teacher I know took advantage of this during one Job from Hell. He reported that not only did it give him peace of mind while he searched for another position, but it helped resolve a few issues in his personal life as well.
- Brainstorm with friends about your options. I know a man who was miserable with his law enforcement job for twenty years. He was at the point of serious health problems but was afraid to quit. Once his friends helped him to acknowledge that his living expenses were low and that he could fall back on some of his retirement fund if necessary, he was able to take the plunge. He later found consulting jobs that were less stressful, and his health improved.
- Give two weeks' notice and take short-term assignments through a temporary staffing service or other avenue until you can find a new job.

Yes, when you have given your one thousand best efforts and it is still the Job from Hell, it may be time to grab your soul—and your coffee cup—and head for the door. Remember the old proverbs: "Every new beginning comes from some other beginning's end" and "Once one door closes behind you, another door of opportunity opens wide." So when you are faced with that moment of truth, remember that other doors will be open soon, and face the truth of moving on.

Chaaaaaaange!

It amazes me how much I still dread change, even after freelancing for more than ten years. You would think I'd be used to it by now, especially since I freely chose this workstyle. But am I? Not exactly. Each time I'm about to embark on a new professional venture—writing a book, taking another contract assignment, teaching a series of workshops, whatever it may be—I experience a terrific storm of nerves. My stomach fills with the proverbial butterflies—not the pretty tropical ones that flutter peacefully around me when I visit the Butterfly Pavilion, but giant skippers, the kind that have three-inch wingspans and fly more than sixty miles per hour.

What's crazy about this is that I actually love change. I thrive on it. In fact, I get restless when I don't get enough. Yet, when faced with a new project, the fear of the unknown takes over, those skippers roar in, and a panicked voice shrieks inside my head: "Argh . . . chaaaaaaange!"

Another crazy thing is that when I get to where I'm going—when the change has been completed—95 percent of the time I'm glad I went there. Still, before I get to this point, I have to deal with the uncertain part of me that resists change. Sound familiar?

These days employment is practically synonymous with change, whether you have a freelance workstyle or one full-time job. Between economic shifts, advancing technology, and corporate restructurings (and re-restructurings), change in the workforce is more prevalent than ever. Add in personal transitions, and some days it's a veritable roller coaster. As a society, we should probably come to expect it. Okay, maybe we *do* expect it. But actually dealing with change is a different matter altogether.

One of the tools I've used over the years to adjust to the constant change in my work is the *I Ching*. Based on the belief system that everything in life eventually evolves, as it does in nature, the *I Ching*, also known as *The Book of Changes*, reminds us that we are ever moving. Even things that appear still are subtly taking on another form. Day gradually turns into night. Spring becomes summer, then fall, then winter, followed by summer again. High tide becomes low tide. And so on, everywhere we look.

Similarly, our human lives naturally change. At work, we begin a project, complete it, then take on something new. We leave one job, find another, then move on to a new position a few years later. In our personal lives, we change our hairstyles, change houses, change the baby's diapers, change the oil in our cars, change our diets, and receive change at the grocery store after paying for our food. We make all of these changes every day. Not only do we make the necessary adjustments, but we succeed quite well.

According to the *I Ching*, to resist this flow of change causes stagnation, whereas going with it results in advancement. Furthermore, through observing, you can begin to predict its motion and apply nature's laws to your own life—including work. At the same time, you can ease transitions by taking a few preparatory steps:

1. *Determine if a change is consonant with your well-being.* Seriously study your options. Sure, it's great to go with the flow, but is this the *right* flow, or are you just changing for the sake of change? Will the grass really be greener on the other side, or might it be brown and full of weeds? I know a medical technician who impulsively quit his job to pursue what sounded like a lucrative network marketing opportunity, only to discover

that the financial gains were sketchy at best. Fortunately, he realized this before it was too late to return to his old job. Later he admitted that the change had definitely not been consonant with either his financial or his emotional well-being.

2. *Make a transforming change.* If you're considering a major change but aren't at a point to make it, try an interim change. This may mean simply taking some mental steps to prepare for what is ahead. When Hannah knew she was going to be leaving her publicity job to attend graduate school full time, she began by emotionally steering away from her current situation. She took her personal belongings home, concentrated more on activities outside of work, and slowly shifted her mental energy toward school. By the time she physically left the job, she was well on her way to completing the transition.

3. *Approach change with careful planning.* This is what Andi did when, at the age of fifty, she retired from the administrative job she had held for twenty-eight years, with the plan to work in a golf course pro shop. On the last day of her old job, she began to prepare for this new career. When she got home, she removed her corporate work outfits from her closet and replaced them with golfing attire, and went away for a celebratory golfing weekend with her husband. The following Monday, Andi wrote cover letters and prepared a résumé outlining her golf experience. The next week, she drove around to all the golf courses in her area, distributing the packets. Within two weeks she had a job.

4. *Consider that timing is of the essence.* Watch carefully to make sure you make the change at the proper time. If you leave too early, you may not be adequately prepared. But if you wait too long, you may miss out on important opportunities. When Andi planned her retirement, it was no coincidence that it was just prior to the opening of golf season in her area. She knew that her new career involved good timing on her part.

5. *Realize that your overall viewpoint may change.* Often when you go through a major transition, your overall viewpoint may

change. Hannah discovered this when she left the commercial publicity world to pursue a master's degree in transpersonal psychology at an alternative college. Suddenly she was in a different environment, focusing on different concerns, and found that she didn't relate to her old life anymore. The change required letting go of old thought patterns, previous activities, and even some longtime friends and associates.

Of course, if the reason you are making a change is because your company is downsizing, you may not have a lot of time to prepare for the transition. But you can still ease yourself through the process. When Thad's company reorganized and he was unsure if his position would be eliminated, he began by accepting a possible change. He reworked his résumé, made contacts at other corporations, and battened down his emotional hatches to prepare for the worst. Meanwhile, realizing that a sense of humor was his best ally, he reserved the video conference center each lunch hour and invited his colleagues to watch comedies. Eventually he did lose his job, but he quickly found another within the same organization—ironically, working for someone who appreciated his capacity to find creative solutions to difficult situations.

INNER VOICES AND MEGAPHONE VOICES

Albert Einstein said his greatest discoveries were revealed through intuition, not logical thinking. Since change is also a form of discovery, listening to your inner voice can be of great benefit throughout the process. For example, let's say your logical voice is telling you to remain in your current work situation because it's the right thing to do, the secure thing to do, but your gut feeling keeps nagging you to make a change. Which do you listen to—the gut feeling or the logical voice?

For most of us, logic operates at a higher volume so it will be heard first, loud and clear. It's as though that voice is holding a megaphone to your ear, squawking, "Damn it, Reginald, stop your whining. I don't care if you always wanted to be a horse trainer. Life insurance is a perfectly respectable business, and retirement is only a thousand years away. What is your problem, man?" Choosing its words carefully, enunciating clearly, the logical voice sounds like the definitive authority. And you think it must be right.

The logical voice is a survival voice, a parental voice that wants to see you safe. Which is great, as long as it doesn't keep you from the realization that you do have choices, as long as it doesn't stop you from hearing an inner voice whispering, "Pssst, Reg, old boy. You know you have the experience and skill to train horses. Why not live life to the fullest and do what you really want to do? Why not make some inquiries and give it a go?"

What I've discovered about logical voices is that they tend to quiet down, to give the inner voice a little leeway when you let them have their say. If you let them scream, yes, screeeeeeeam, as I used to do with my class many years ago when I taught preschool. On days when the children were very excited and the volume of that excitement was getting on adult nerves, I would herd them into a room, close the door, and encourage them all to express themselves loudly for a full five minutes. I can still see their adrenaline running, their tiny bodies jumping up and down in an effort to make their voices louder. Usually after three or four minutes, however, they were tired of the game and more than willing to return to what my mother always called "a dull roar."

Megaphone voices are the same way. After they have had their say, they are often happy to settle down to a dull roar. At which point your deeper voice, your gravelly, gut-level, this-is-what-I-*really*-want-to-do voice, can have its turn.

ENVISION THE CHANGE

Change is a little like a New Year of the soul. It's like leaving all your old stuff in the year of the past, accepting a glass of dry champagne, and stepping out on the dance floor with someone new. Since, as the *I Ching* says, "Change only inspires confidence after it is accomplished, after there is long-range visibility," sometimes it helps to envision the change.

This is what my friend Kate did after she was let go from her seventy-hour-a-week executive job at a national magazine, with no idea of what to do next. Of course, her megaphone voice was yelling its head off for her to trot herself right back down the avenue and apply pronto to another magazine, but Kate couldn't bring herself to do it. Instead, she decided to check into alternative routes.

After Kate's megaphone voice gave up on her and huffed off in search of a new victim, Kate slowed down and focused on experiencing life sans overtime for the first time since college. She got really, really quiet and conserved her mental energy. She took long walks and observed the world around her. And slowly she began to envision her change.

First Kate imagined herself letting go of her old job, leaving it in the year of the past. Next she accepted that glass of champagne—metaphorically speaking—and flowed through the transitions she had made since the day she left the job. She continued to watch herself flow as she began to visualize what she might do next, using her experience and her skills. Publication work of a different nature? Freelance writing? Teaching? These were all possibilities, and she imagined herself flowing toward each one. As Kate allowed her imagination to drift, she saw herself traveling to her new office at her new job, perhaps in a different city. She envisioned her new job duties, her new boss, her new colleagues, and everything that would happen when the change was over. Finally she felt herself flowing with it all. She could see herself successfully moving on.

In Kate's case, she literally did move—back to her hometown where, by "coming full circle," she felt that she could make a fresh start. At first she wasn't certain what that start would be, but it was a step. After exploring a variety of options, she found a teaching position at the local university. In retrospect, Kate realizes that she accomplished major changes through envisioning her final success.

GO OUT ON A LIMB

Sometimes when I'm about to make a change, I envision myself going out on a limb. Just a little. Okay, maybe more. I see myself taking one step and then another, balancing carefully until I'm at the very end. So what if the bough breaks and I fall into the river below? It may wake me up and let me know that my swimming techniques are more advanced than I think. What if the bough *doesn't* break? I might get to the end of the limb and find the god of jobs waiting in all her crowned glory. Maybe she will say, "What the heck took you so long? Boy, do I have some great news for you!"

Either way, by going out on that limb, I have opened up my possibilities. I have initiated a change that may even result in a major breakthrough.

So, even though I may dread change, I remind myself to get out on the limb. To get past the giant skippers roaring around in my stomach, to listen to my inner voice and envision a change when it's time. I tell myself to work past "Argh . . . chaaaaaaange!" and instead to reflect upon another *I Ching* wisdom: "When the way comes to an end, then change—having changed, you pass through."

CHANGING CAREERS

BURK, A seventh-grade teacher, is on his third career since receiving his B.A. fifteen years ago. Although he immediately found work in his field—legal research—it quickly became clear that this wasn't his life work. A temporary administrative job became his second career and another dead end. Finally, through realizing his fulfilling experiences as a father and coaching children's sports, he earns a certificate to teach.

Sonia, a computer programmer seeking a change in career, discovers through volunteering at the local community food share gardens that she wants to be an organic gardener. She enters a two-year organic gardening apprenticeship program that is reviewed in a trade publication and subsequently organizes a cooperative farm with several others from the program.

Johnson, a Zen teacher with an M.A. in social sciences, has been making his living as a carpenter for more than twenty years because it helped the Zen community and offered him the flexibility to continue his Buddhist studies. When he injures his back, making construction work an impossibility, he arranges a trade-out with a Zen student who is a psychotherapist. Thus, he enters the psychotherapy profession through an exchange for advanced meditation instruction.

————————————

Wren, a bookstore manager, is looking for a challenge beyond her current job. Using her skills and knowledge of the book industry, she takes a little sidestep—into the mail order department of a book publisher—and thus creates a new career for herself. Over the next five years, she learns everything that she can, and grows with the business. Her resourcefulness eventually pays off when her manager leaves the company, and she easily steps up into his position.

————————————

Now that you are a master of change, here comes the big one: changing careers. Have you been restless professionally for quite some time? Are you ready to do something different or more meaningful with your work? Are external circumstances nudging you in a new direction? As the four people in these vignettes discovered, it may be time.

Why change? I hear a wide range of reasons. Some people, like Sonia, hope to work away from the "just a job" syndrome and toward something that offers deeper satisfaction, and a chance to make a stronger community contribution. Many, like Wren, enjoy their work, but want to be challenged beyond their current positions. Johnson and others face situations beyond their control, such as injury or downsizing, that forces them to make an unintended but often welcome transition.

And then there are those like Burk, who find that what they originally trained for isn't ultimately what they want to do ten or twenty years later. Which isn't a big surprise. I mean, how do you know at the age of eighteen or nineteen what you want to do for the rest of your life? How do you know that you won't find other interests down the road? Personally, when I was eighteen, my priorities were poetry, sex, and Mozart, and not necessarily in that order. It didn't occur to me to be overly concerned with a lifelong career.

Burk is among the many, many people I've met in recent years who are making complete shifts in their careers. Indeed, statistics show that professionals are changing careers—not just jobs—more than ever, often three or four times within the course of their working life. And why not change? Why not do a little occupational metamorphosis from time to time? Why not trade in science for massage therapy, monkhood for novel writing, or catering for buffoonery if you have the chance? (Don't laugh. Professional clown schools have long been in existence and buffoonery is considered to be a very noble profession.) Why not retire from a thirty-year career as a Canadian Mountie and begin a second career in real estate? You might even follow the lead of one of my cyber-colleagues who sold his occult bookstore and returned to his original track of civil engineering. Whatever your plan, changing careers may be the very best thing for keeping your productivity and creativity alive.

While many fields require the standard step of returning to school for a relevant degree, it is possible to redirect occupational interests using other innovative methods—without making a large investment in time or financials. Here are a few examples of what I've seen.

APPRENTICESHIPS

Apprenticing is an age-old and practical way to launch yourself into a new career. An apprenticeship is hands-on training with a professional in the field, in lieu of a classroom, although it could be in addition to a related degree. Traditionally, the apprentice receives a small stipend for his work—at a lower wage than an experienced employee could expect, since much of the pay is in learning the trade. For this reason, many apprentices do this training in addition to their current job or make arrangements with their present employers to work part-time hours while learning their new trade. Either way, the clear advantage of an apprenticeship is that the apprentice receives important experience in addition to skills and education—all of which more smoothly pave the way to a new career.

An apprenticeship can be a full-time program, as in the case of Sonia's organic gardening course, in which her work covered room and board while she paid tuition for the actual training. It might be a more traditional one-on-one situation, as with my friend David, a violin maker and restorer who learned his trade from a master violin maker in Germany. Or it may be more of a reciprocal scenario, such as Johnson's creative trade-out.

Over the years I've worked with several people in a variety of fields who came to their professions through apprenticeships— among them a photojournalist, a publication designer, a social worker, a psychotherapist, an aesthetician, several organic farmers, a chef, a dental assistant and even a lawyer. How did they find their teachers? Through professional and personal contacts, the Yellow Pages, trade magazines, professional directories, community directories, the Internet, adult education classes and workshops, serendipity, and a lot of personal perseverance.

One word of caution: In seeking an apprenticeship, thoroughly check out your sources to make sure the program is authentic. Get recommendations from working professionals and from other apprentices who have attended the courses. While the majority of programs are valid, I've heard of a few that are only expensive and not very informational workshops, designed to make money for the facilitators.

COMMUNITY WORK

You can always add to your knowledge base, but experience is the key in today's working world. As the old adage has it, knowledge is power. And experience combined with knowledge is powerful.

Keeping this in mind, you can see that community work is another excellent way to move into a new field, since it provides both relevant experience and employment contacts. Alice, a bookkeeper, took advantage of both when she decided to turn her lifetime love of animals into a career. First, she volunteered in a veterinarian's office to gain some hands-on experience and to make sure this was the direction she wanted to take. After deciding that, yes, this was the path for her, she enrolled in a formal university course of veterinary technical training, while continuing to volunteer and to hold down her bookkeeping job.

It was an amazing amount of work, Alice later admitted. In fact, there were times when she wondered if she should have gone to clown school instead; at least, as she put it, she would have had a few more laughs. Ultimately, it *was* worth it. Three years later, she was able to work her way into a full-time veterinary position, finally transitioning herself into her new and fulfilling career.

I know a number of others who have found new careers this way—among them a fund-raiser for a Native American advocacy organization, an architectural preservation historian, and a preschool teacher. After all, just about any field lends itself to volunteer work in some capacity, and most businesses welcome volunteers. Contacts can be made through a community volunteer clearing house, or you can approach companies directly.

CERTIFICATE PROGRAMS AND THE INTERNET

Of course, returning to school and obtaining a relevant degree is an obvious way to change careers—or even to step into a more advanced level of your current business. This was true for my pharmacist friend Carrie, who required a doctoral degree to move out of the pharmacy and into her new area of drug information research. On the other hand, Lauren, a computer technician, found that a less rigorous certificate program in Geographical Information Systems (GIS) at a local university was an effective step toward a new career.

Similar programs are available in numerous fields and are offered through avenues such as universities and the Internet. I met a surgeon who could no longer perform surgery after she was diagnosed with multiple sclerosis. However, she could still work, and she wished to stay in the medical field. So she enrolled in a series of courses in hospital administration through the Internet and used her training to move into a new career.

Certificate programs are smart educational alternatives because they generally require less time and money to complete than degree programs do. They are often self-paced, making it easier to combine them with an already full-time work load. A more formal degree can always be completed later. I know several professionals who have worked their way via certificate into an entry-level job in their new field. Later, their employers were willing to contribute to their education costs and, in some cases, even offered promotions.

WHICH DIRECTION SHOULD YOU TAKE?

All of these folks knew the careers they wanted to pursue. But what if you aren't sure which way to go? What if you just wish the employment wizards would conjure up a career with your name on it and send it via magic carpet or at least Fedex overnight? Unfortunately, I haven't witnessed too many instances of this phenomenon. There are a few other options:

1. *Take a look at what endures.* Education, criminal justice, and service industries (catering, personal care, child care, transportation, etc.) are a few fields that are omnipresent in the workforce. Ed, a telecommunications professional I know, kept this in mind when he changed his career to law enforcement. Legal services, recreation, and entertainment, including

the aforementioned ancient art of buffoonery, are other areas that endure.

2. *Keep apprised of rapid growth areas.* According to current U.S. Department of Labor statistics, health services, business services, and social services will account for the most job growth over the next several years. This includes the medical field—and consider how many areas this involves. And as our society becomes more open to the body-mind connection and spirituality in the workplace, alternative medicine practices and metaphysical-based businesses are also on the rise—and there is also a higher demand for the services of such professionals as astrologers and energetic healers.

3. *Consider skills that can be applied to a number of professions.* These include computer work of all kinds, education, research, accounting, and both feature and technical writing, among others. Valerie tapped into this possibility when she found freelance accounting assignments with a hatha-yoga collective and a Buddhist meditation center.

4. *Check out the professions of people you know.* Think of your friends, family members, neighbors, people in your book club, and in your aikido class. Does anyone have a profession that you are especially drawn to? Have you considered your sister's colleague's Uncle Waldo the taxidermist? Have you thought about your mysterious neighbor who lives down the block? You don't know exactly what she does for a living but whatever it is takes her frequently to the greengrocer. You see her walking past your house several times each day, hauling kohlrabi, basil, huge antlers of ginger root, bags of garlic and all sorts of other tasty treats. If you are a great fan of the greengrocer yourself, her line of work may be of interest to you. Maybe you could "interview" these people to find out more about their jobs. Perhaps they would even be willing to act as mentors, providing contacts and advice.

5. *Investigate your special interests.* Love to snowboard and mountain bike? Go into partnership with some fellow boarders and

open a specialty shop. Always been interested in holistic health? Train to be an acupuncturist or a chiropractor. Take a close look at your other personal passions. You may be closer to a new career than you think.

6. *Brainstorm.* Keeping in mind the proverb, "If you only look at what is, you might never attain what could be," do some vigorous brainstorming. Sit around the dinner table with your family, your friends, your goldfish, or boa constrictor, and toss a few thoughts back and forth. Dare to be wild. Is it so far-fetched to join the Peace Corps in Malaysia for a year or more? Could you possibly teach English in Japan (or Romania or the Ukraine), as a number of my friends have done? Ask longtime friends what they can imagine for you. When Roberto, a dissatisfied climatologist, did this, he was surprised to find that his friends imagined him as a massage therapist. The more he considered the idea, the more he liked it. Eventually he took their suggestion.

7. *Pay attention to your dreams.* Marie-Louise von Franz said: "Dreams show us how to find meaning in our lives, how to fulfill our own destiny, how to realize the greater potential of life within us." So activate your dream agenda and direct it toward finding a new career. Your subconscious may be working on a secret scheme, as many career changers discover, much to their delight. Try keeping a dream journal by your bed. Before you go to sleep each night, give your subconscious the agenda of working on your new career. As soon as you have a dream, write it down. Give it several weeks or months because your inner self may be shy. After it trusts you enough to open up, anything can happen. And probably will.

8. *Check in with a reputable astrologer or psychic.* While you're recording your dreams, see if a psychic or astrology reading can offer any clues. My mother, a forty-year telephone company veteran, visited a woman whom she called "The Witch" a few years before she retired. The reading gave her several important insights into both her current job situation and sub-

sequent retirement. Similarly, I consult with Alex, a Vedic astrologer, for guidance in determining career moves. "While astrology won't reveal specific job titles," Alex says, "it can point out your particular potentials to be in the right place at the right time." Using ancient techniques to work with the planetary periods in my chart, Alex has offered several accurate predictions that have helped me not only in my career, but in other areas of my life as well.

You might also "serve up your wish to the Universe," as some of my friends say, in the possibility that serendipity will present its own plan. Hundreds of people discover vocations completely by happenstance, as with an administrator associate of mine who coincidentally met her true calling as a lawyer after becoming involved in a sexual harassment lawsuit against her employer. She won the suit, which paid her way through law school. She is now a lawyer, specializing in—guess what?—sexual harassment cases.

Another acquaintance found his new career in a similar way. Having aimlessly wandered the employment road for years, he had just about given up on finding the right match when he read a newspaper story about an alternative radio station that offered free training sessions for disc jockeys in exchange for volunteer DJ services. Since he had an extensive knowledge of music and a true media personality, he enrolled in the classes. After graduating and working as a volunteer for several months, he eventually moved to a larger city and netted a DJ job in a commercial radio station. Which goes to show that serendipity does have its way.

Whether you choose an apprenticeship, a certificate program, are working with your dreams, or are still waiting for your big break, being on the brink of a career change can be a very exciting time. Just keep your eyes open and concentrate on getting some new experiences into your life as you search. New careers can—and do—appear out of the blue.

DOWNSIZED? WHAT NEXT?

AN ENGINEER who was let go from his job at a high-tech company told me he felt like he had been galloping at a hundred miles an hour when he arrived unexpectedly at a cliff with a sheer drop-off of ten thousand feet. Of course, he had no choice but to come to a screeching halt, but then what? After twenty years with the same organization, the same position, the same colleagues, he couldn't imagine being anywhere else. Still, he couldn't go back to where he started from, so he stood there waiting and wondering, What next?

"It was hard not to take it personally, even though sixty other managers were also let go," Ben admitted. "They gave us two weeks to clean out our offices and say our good-byes, so I had some time to get used to it, but what got me was the day my access card was deactivated. I had to enter the building like any other visitor, like I didn't belong. It was a real shock. That's when I saw myself at the edge of the cliff."

I have heard similar reports from others whose jobs have been eliminated: "I feel like a shark out of water." "I got painted out of the picture." "The clock in my office wound all the way down."

And more dramatically, from a friend who is a corporate spy and midnight novelist, "I was almost at the top when the volcano began to erupt and my job got offered to the volcano gods."

The analogies vary, but the idea is the same—that sudden stopgap with what at first seems like nothing to do, nowhere to go, no foreseeable source of income, and a great chasm of time to fill. All things combined, it can be a major shock. Or, as Ben saw it, a major cliff.

Certainly it's an enormous transition from working forty or more hours a week to not working at all. To being between jobs. As a society of doers, a culture of go-getters, being in limbo isn't something that comes easily to most of us. Typically, we are programmed to be productive, to be constantly moving forward, so how can we imagine that standstill in any form could lead anywhere, let alone to success? Not only that, but as we stand there, hurricanes of uninvited emotions descend upon us when we least expect it. No wonder we don't want to stay still.

When Ben's position was surplussed, he found himself going quickly through the emotional phases that typically accompany a job loss—anger, hurt, denial, regret, bitterness, sadness, worry. Although he passed through most of them fairly quickly, the phase he kept getting mired in was denial.

"As much as I tried to believe it, I just couldn't," he told me several months later. "I couldn't accept that it was over. It took weeks and weeks. When I finally saw that I couldn't go back, it hit me so hard that it was like a part of me had literally died. My life seemed to loom before me and a lot of questions came up, including what is my life about, anyway? Right now that seems melodramatic, but the feelings were very strong at the time."

FINDING YOUR BALANCE

Everyone has his or her own method for handling a job loss. Some talk it over with family and friends. A few take long hikes, go on a trip, or work on projects previously left on hold. Some begin the employment application process right away because they don't want to lose their momentum. Others sign up for unemployment benefits, take a rest, and take their time.

One way I've found to deal with a between-job period is to take the Taoist viewpoint that life is a series of high and low cycles, the secret of life being to find a balance between the two. That by balancing the high and low cycles that are inevitable in our world and equalizing the extremes in our lives, we can realize peace and success.

Taoist Master Hua-Ching Ni says of this, "Sometimes you do better in life and other times you do poorly. When your cycle is high, you enjoy your life more than when you are having difficulties in a low cycle. To harmonize the flow of your life, do not become excited by the high points or depressed by the low ones. Always remember, the high is built by the low."

So when you find yourself between jobs, you might consider that you have entered a low period, a short time of rest that precedes another high. Since a low cycle is typically marked by less energy, it's a time to stop and collect your mental and physical reserves. This means getting more sleep and engaging in quieter activities such as watching movies, reading, or sitting down and writing out your options, as I like to do. It might mean staying in bed for a month and reading travel books, as my friend Tina did after her last job ended. Or going on an extended Zen retreat, as Valerie did after a high-stress freelance assignment came to an end. A low cycle is a time to do whatever you can do to give yourself a break, to rebuild.

A job hiatus is an opportunity to regroup, to consider, "What next?" This might manifest as getting other areas of your life back in order, focusing on family and activities that may have previously taken a backseat to your work. It could be your first chance in years to have time to reflect on what else you want to do with your life beyond how you've been living. However you use the time, the more you allow yourself to recharge your energy, the smoother will be the transition into the next cycle.

MAKING THE TRANSITION

A corporate consultant I spoke with says that the key to working with transition is understanding that it is a process, not an event.

An event, she explains, is something that occurs within a finite period of time and is quickly over—been there, done that. A process, on the other hand, is ongoing, taking weeks, months, or even years to work through.

Part of working with the process is realizing that the peaks and valleys will overlap. You may have a burst of energy, move forward, feel like you are moving toward an all-time high, and imagine that the valley is behind you forever, only to find yourself suddenly slowing down again. During a job transition, this happens several times, with the slower periods growing shorter and shorter, until you make the transition from valley to peak.

After the first period of adjustment, you may be ready to increase your momentum by applying for unemployment benefits if you haven't done so already, putting personal financials in order, and determining the next step. Will you shortly begin the networking and application process? Will you do contract work until you decide on a new direction? If you received a generous severance package, will you take time off . . . return to school . . . change careers? Will you travel or start your own business? There are so many options.

If your plan is to launch back into the job search, there is good news. According to a recent survey by Challenge, Gray & Christmas, a Chicago-based outplacement firm, "Ninety percent of downsized managers and professionals find jobs with equal or better pay within three months." Of course, three months may seem like an enormous gap when you are between jobs, but it is actually a relatively short period in the grand scheme of a career.

Several acquaintances of mine bridge the gap by working on a consulting or contract basis until new jobs come through. Others use the time to make connections at career expos and job-related workshops and through the Internet. A particularly enterprising magazine editor, who left her position because of what she termed "supremely bad chemistry," had cards printed up representing herself as Editor-at-Large. She distributed them to all the publishing contacts she knew and used her downtime to work freelance assignments—a scheme that eventually netted her a full-time job.

TAKE ADVANTAGE OF THE FREE TIME

After you take a few measures toward finding a new job, make a list of what you can do to use the free time to your advantage. Do you have projects on hold? Is there a special subject you've been meaning to read up on? Is there something you've always wanted to do but were never quite able to make time for? This may be the perfect time.

One woman I know, angry after being let go in a political struggle at her public relations firm, bulldozed her energy into large projects around her house. First she steam-cleaned the carpets, painted old bookshelves, and organized the garage. Next she had a yard sale and gave the unsold items to Goodwill. As her momentum increased, she gave the garden a thorough weeding, put in flowers, and even planted an oak—a symbol to herself that she was as strong as that venerable tree.

Imagine what a sense of accomplishment this woman had when she was finished. On a psychological level, letting go of old projects helped her to release old resentments and cleared the air for new ventures. Creating something wonderful for herself (the garden and tree) gave her a sense of renewal before heading for new horizons. Horizons that were indeed realized when she found a position at a rival company two months later.

Andrew, an ESL teacher, experienced a similar sense of renewal after his job loss. But instead of focusing on his domestic area, he tapped into the greater community by using the extra time in his job search period to volunteer in a nursing home. Although the work didn't bring in a salary, he reported that it helped him feel reconnected, as well as reminding him that there were many other work situations beyond the job he just left. Plus he found an unexpected benefit in that another ESL associate was among his fellow volunteers, which gave him some job contacts in the process.

VIEW THIS TIME AS VACATION

Who knows when you will have this kind of time again, so why not use a few of the hours for pure enjoyment? Do some of the things you couldn't do if you had a full-time job. Go to a matinee or a baseball game. Take a short road trip or be a tourist in your own town. Go to a museum that you rarely get to, visit the zoo, or ride on the swan boats in the city park.

Or catch up with yourself on a personal level, as one of my friends likes to do when she is between jobs. Get a haircut, make an appointment for a complete physical, get a massage, or swim afternoon laps at the Y. She says that even if she doesn't feel motivated in the beginning, she always ends up thanking herself later when she feels rejuvenated and appears refreshed during those important interviews.

Speaking of feeling refreshed, when was the last time you had a good laugh? While Ben was trying to figure out "what next?" he decided to lighten up by renting funny movies, reading humorous essays, and enjoying Dr. Seuss books with his four-year-old nephew. After a while, he truly felt like he was on a planned vacation. Sometimes laughter *is* the best medicine.

If nothing else, maybe this is the time to fulfill a dream. Start writing the novel that's been scratching at the back door of your mind, barking to get in. Dust off the family genealogy charts you've been planning to research. Get some French tapes and practice your conversation skills in anticipation of a long-desired trip to Paris. You never know when you will have the time again. Whatever your dream, how about making it happen *now*?

Getting back to Ben, he ended up using his time to fulfill his own dream, using his severance pay to open a used bookstore with a friend—a business they had been talking about starting for a long time. Now as he shelves books and waits on customers, he looks back on being at the edge of that cliff and thinks it was actually a blessing in disguise. Yes, it was, he says, because if it hadn't happened, he probably wouldn't have experienced the valley period of his life that inspired the change.

Truly, the high is built by the low.

Getting
Inspired
Again

THE PSYCHOLOGY OF
WORKING AT HOME

HANDS DOWN, the question I'm asked most about working at home is if I remain in my bathrobe all day. No kidding. It happens at parties, on contract jobs, on airplanes, anywhere I happen to mention my particular workstyle. I'll go to teach a workshop, a hand will shoot up, and twenty minutes later I'll realize I've been discussing something decidedly not on my agenda—the details of my workaday attire. Finally, at one workshop, I asked why there was so much curiosity about what home-based workers wear when they work at home.

The responses were varied.

One woman said, "If I worked at home, I would never ever get dressed. I mean, why bother? I wondered if you felt the same way."

Another person said that ever since he saw the *Dilbert* cartoon on telecommuting, he imagined all home workers sitting at their computers, clad in nothing but a floating tie.

A third person enlightened me further. "I've already read the books on how to set up a business. What I want to understand is how you actually *do* it day by day. How being on your own affects you and how you handle it. You know, the psychology of working at home."

The more she talked, the more I saw that people wanted a specific image. They wanted to visualize *what it actually looked like*, this alternative to working in a corporate office. They weren't after the hard-core business aspects—most had tapped into the many fine related books on the market—but they did want what I saw as the tedious details of how I fit together the little pieces of my day. They wanted to see the completed puzzle of a real person at work in a real home setting. As the woman explained it: the psychology of working at home.

The sticky wicket of psychology is that everyone is different. And the thing about being house-based is that there are no set policies as there often are in a large corporation. Add in the fact that more than forty-five million workers do at least some of their work on the home front, and there is probably a special method, a unique psychology, for every person with this workstyle. So while I can answer questions about how I operate, *Dilbert* or Zelda Wigglesworth or any number of others will most likely respond otherwise. There are probably forty-five million (and then some) psychologies of working at home.

This disclaimer aside, I will say that I know a stockbroker who wears a full three-piece suit to his attic office every morning and a book designer who dresses in a skirt in her garage studio, but then, yes, I can think of a few folks who keep their apparel to a bare minimum. As for myself, I may work in my bathrobe for the first hour or two while my thoughts are waking up, but then I get dressed for the rest of the day. Oh, nothing quite so formal as a suit or a dress, mind you, but there is something about the preparation of getting ready for work, albeit in yoga-style clothes, a loose work shirt and leggings, that gets me in the proper frame of mind for work. For me, getting dressed is fairly important; it reminds me that I am really working and not just acting out a role.

On the other hand, I do have a friend, a romance writer named Isabel, who not only works in her nightgown but in bed. She has been doing this for probably twenty years, although I think she has an office somewhere else in her house. She has her computer and preprogrammed coffeemaker bedside and goes to work as soon as she wakes up, usually around six. As she says, what could be more appropriate than writing a romance in bed? It helps her keep the proper frame of mind.

When she has "pounded out the chapter of the day," as she affectionately describes it, she gets up and goes about the next chapter of her life. Generally, this is around two in the afternoon, but it could be noon or four or even six—depending on the complexity of the scene-of-the-day and if her characters are feeling cooperative.

SELF-DISCIPLINE

The next most frequently asked question I get about working at home is how I manage self-discipline when there are oh-so-many interesting distractions. Excellent question. I mean, what could be more exciting than cleaning out that messy utility closet? What could be more alluring than repotting the squirrel-foot fern? And how could you possibly work when the latest psychothriller novel is screaming at you to put aside your work and find out who done it?

In short, people ask, how do you get the work done with all those distractions and nobody telling you what to do?

I have two approaches to this. First, I take the view that I am the boss and I am the employee. I tell myself what to do and then I do it. I know it sounds a little schizophrenic, but it does work—especially when I get to work first thing in the morning. Second, I remind myself that discipline is a matter of pure survival. If I can't discipline myself to do the work, I won't be very productive, let alone successful. If I don't sit down in front of that computer, I tell myself, I won't get much of anywhere at all. And let's face it, unless I'm visited by sudden leprechauns bearing huge pots of gold, money is going to be a bit of a problem.

My friend Isabel has discipline down pat. In a word, she is ruthless. No gimmicks for her. Her rule is that she remains in bed until her chapter is completed, no excuses. The way she sees it, she is at work and work equals discipline, plain and simple. She signs her book contracts four at a time, so there is a lot of work (and discipline) ahead of her. She does have two exceptions to the rule: trips to the bathroom and if the dog catches on fire.

Unless I'm close to deadline, I'm not quite so strict (which is probably why Isabel has fifty books in print and I have only five). Oh, I guess in the beginning I found that the work was better enforced with a few practicalities such as an office separate from the rest of my home, beginning each day with a ritual (nothing elaborate, just a few minutes of deep breathing, followed by one strong cup of organic Sumatran), and creating a fairly strict schedule. But after finding my inner rhythms, I found that I did better with a varying schedule, that the creative process demanded some give and take. So I settled into the rhythm of giving in to the distractions rather than fighting them, and interweaving my professional and personal selves through each day. Generally, it looks like this: write a little . . . put a thought on hold and consider it while I weed the yarrow garden; write a little more . . . go for a walk; write . . . pick some cosmos and arrange them in the cobalt vase; write some more . . . call a friend, figure out what to make for dinner. And so on. A different tapestry every day.

On a more serious note, lest you think me la-dee-dah, I do average six to eight hours of solid work (six hours of working at home being easily equal to eight hours of working in a corporate setting, where there are far more interruptions), usually in two-hour intervals, somewhere between seven A.M. and seven P.M. By this time—unless I'm on deadline, in which case I work all hours of the day and night—my husband has arrived home and I'm ready to relax, have dinner, and put work on hold for the night.

ADVANTAGES AND CHALLENGES

When I tell people that I work at home, I notice that there is an even division between the work-at-home wannabes and those who wouldn't do it in a million trillion years. The wannabes are drawn to the advantages, notably the flexibility factors: the freedom to wear a red silk bathrobe all day and make your own schedule; the famous thirty-second commute; and the comfort of knowing that there is no boss in sight barking orders at any given hour of the day.

The would-never-bes could not care less about these so-called perks. They prefer what a corporate friend of mine calls "the separation of church and work," a clear boundary between personal and workaday lives. These folks would rather let their employers worry about the itty bitty gritty business details, including health insurance and tax deductions. They like the idea of building up their corporate-provided benefits packages. If they could, they wouldn't even want to *tele*commute. For them, the actual commute is their private space for organizing thoughts, listening to National Public Radio, and talking out loud about how they might change the world in eighty-eight days. As for the red silk bathrobe, it just isn't an issue; these folks wouldn't be caught dead in a red bathrobe if it were the last piece of clothing on earth.

Those who might like to try their hand at working at home don't seem terribly concerned about the challenges of having to market themselves constantly to keep up a steady work flow (and cash flow), paying their own benefits and taxes, and effectively managing their own time. Because, realistically, they plan to build a safe reserve before their home-based business is launched; they have the funds to cover start-up costs; and they are generally self-starters to begin with. If their plan is to telecommute, they have the details worked out with their employers prior to entering into the arrangement. They already have their bases covered.

The wannabes have their bases covered on the domestic front, too. They know there is bound to be some overlap of personal and business lives, and they are willing to be flexible with both sets of needs. They aren't too concerned about "little surprises" that may occur in a home operation, such as when the cat raids the laundry basket and drags three pairs of dirty underwear into your office just as you and a client are signing an important contract. Instead, they think, "Oh well, these things happen." They are willing to work with whatever comes up.

At this point, the wannabes are mainly viewing the whole package as an opportunity to create a little more professional freedom. "Hey, the benefits are the flexibility and variety, right?" they say. "The perks are doing what you want to do, *n'est-ce pas? Vive la independence!*"

While the wannabes are toasting what they see as a liberated workstyle, those who say "no way" to working at home ask, "How *do* you keep your business separate from your personal life? Isn't that a disadvantage?"

Maybe it is and maybe it isn't, depending on your workstyle and your personality. Val, a Russian translator friend who works out of his house, finds it easier to concentrate when he draws a clear line, which he accomplishes by simply closing his office door when he is "at work." This indicates to friends and family that he is unavailable in the same way as he would be if he were at a nine-to-five job across town. At the end of the day, he opens his office door, meaning that he is home. To further delineate the division, Val's office is near the front door, well away from the rest of the house. This helps to define boundaries for visiting clients and ensures that the business doesn't infringe upon other family members who may be home at the time.

Whereas Val finds that this is the only way he can operate at home, I know others who simply set up home businesses and blend it all together, not thinking much about the overlap. As one friend points out, "Why not mix it up? After all, we are an integration of everything we do. Nothing is black and white."

Being a writer, I know a lot of other writers, and many of them share this philosophy. They are always talking about the chapters they wrote with babies on their laps, the newsletters that got done with cats on their keyboards, the stories that got started on the bathroom tiles with soap crayons while giving the dog or the kids (or both) a bath. Even with the circus happening all around them, they just keep writing. They make their work one of the acts.

A couple who cross-train Japanese and Americans on cultural business practices have a similar approach. They host Japanese visitors in their guest rooms, are accompanied by their two young children when they give seminars across the country and in Japan, and often socialize with clients and their families when on Japanese tours. To balance it out, they return phone calls during nap times or when the kids are at off-site play groups, and much of their work is packed into the few hours after the children's bedtime. As they say, flex-time is definitely the order here. So far they have found few conflicts in their methods—especially since they set aside a number of weeks a year that are strictly for family, when the business is "shut down" and personal lives rule.

BUILDING A WORK COMMUNITY

One final question I often hear about working at home is, "Do you ever feel isolated?" To which my romance-writer friend would quip, "Isolated? How could I, with these characters acting up all the time?" Isabel views her solitary writing situation as a veritable gathering, her work life as practically a party, but many home workers, myself included, do sometimes combat a sense of operating out of the loop. For this reason, when I'm working at home, I find it necessary to establish my own work community, not only for personal rapport, but for the purposes of brainstorming, moral support, and increasing the momentum that occurs more easily when nudged by social contact.

After pooling ideas with a few colleagues about how to build community, we came up with the following list:

• Create a network of colleagues who work at home. They could be friends, neighbors, former coworkers, parents of your children's friends, or home-based workers from your Wednesday morning tai chi class. Get together once or twice a week for lunch or coffee and keep in touch by telephone.

- Join a group of small-business owners. Often these groups are listed in newspapers, advertised in flyers on bulletin boards, and registered with a local chamber of commerce.
- Work one morning a week in a park or café. Just being out of the house and in the world generates a feeling of connectedness. You will likely meet people who have similar schedules, some of whom will become part of your network.
- Create a virtual community by keeping in touch with friends and associates through E-mail or fax. In this way, your community can be truly global. I regularly connect with a cyber group of writers. We share ideas, give and receive feedback on our work, and generally provide moral support. I also take Internet classes and attend interactive lectures on a variety of topics from herbal medicine to astrology. With so much activity, I feel much less isolated.
- Get out at least once each day for luncheons, coffee dates, or walks. Initiate brief conversations with people you encounter on your round of errands. Chat with library and grocery store employees (an exchange could be as simple as "Great morning, isn't it?"). Have friends over for dinner more often.
- Make the community at large your work community. Volunteer in a soup kitchen or deliver meals-on-wheels over the lunch hour. Spend a few hours a week as a Big Brother or Big Sister or visit a resident in a nursing home. One of the advantages of business at home is that you have the flexibility to integrate these activities into the workday.
- Establish a business that requires frequent interactions. My neighbor Elizabeth, a very people-oriented network marketer of Japanese health products, finds that she spends so much time with clients, others marketers, and distributors that she actually

has more social contacts than when she worked full time as a social worker in the public schools.

After you've been working at home for a while, community may occur naturally with people who share your workstyle. You see them in the grocery store during off hours and on walks in the park after everyone else has gone to work. They are the ones in midmorning yoga classses and early afternoon lap swims at the Y. If you see these people often enough you may strike up a conversation and happily find that you have more in common than just the fact that you work at home.

Some of these folks may even live on your street, as I discovered about my neighborhood a few years ago. This informal immediate community supports my work and offers a sense of rapport. A few times a week I walk with Elizabeth or have tea with my sculptor friend Helen. We have impromptu driveway discussions with other neighbors as I work in the garden or walk to the mailbox. Such simple encounters create some extra light in the daily routine. Also, it's good to have other professionals nearby with whom to brainstorm as well as projects outside of my own work to consider.

My neighborhood work community occurred by coincidence, but come to think of it, a deliberate working neighborhood might be a worthwhile living plan for home business owners. It could provide a valuable social network and a "watchdog" exchange for when people travel. This system might be set up for pooling resources and services to save time, money, and energy for everyone. With trends toward quality family time, more simple lifestyles, and a concern for the environment, more and more there is a high incentive to make such a situation work.

Of course, chemistry being volatile as it is, it's best to set a few boundaries in working neighborhoods, to ensure that the community doesn't become a serious distraction or an invasion of privacy. Arrangements such as predetermined break times and telephone calls rather than sudden appearances on each other's doorsteps can go a long way toward creating community success.

HOW DO YOU KNOW IF IT'S FOR YOU?

As advanced technology and the growth of smaller business networks make this workstyle attractive to a larger segment of the population, the number of home-based workers sky-rockets. According to a recent Harvard Business School survey, 33 percent of those in the class of 1983 had become self-employed within five years of graduation—19 percent more graduates than in 1978. Other random surveys report that someone becomes a home-based worker every sixteen seconds, through either establishing a business or telecommuting. Yes, I said *seconds*, which I personally find difficult to believe, but sometimes I am a skeptic when it comes to statistics. Whether it's seconds or minutes or even hours, working at home is definitely one of the hot work alternatives. But how do you know if it's for you?

If you are considering a business move to the home, you might see if you match up with the following qualities (compiled from a number of surveys—the ones I'm *not* skeptical about):

- Independent in your thinking
- Results oriented
- Confident (high self-esteem)
- Self-reliant
- A good listener
- Highly professional and ethical
- Knowledge-seeking
- Technologically savvy
- Able to anticipate and manage problems
- Versatile and flexible
- Able to take on the mundane tasks along with the more creative aspects of the job

If you nodded emphatically to the majority of qualities on this list, working at home may be for you. It means that you have a successful product or service that sells . . . are realistic about cash flow . . . have no problem working alone . . . and are willing to clock in the long, hard hours necessary for success. It also means that you can "separate church and work," that you have the technology to get the job, and that you are able to do most of the work yourself. Or, in my case, all of the work myself. While I was writing this chapter I gave section assignments to two of my colleagues. But do you think these colleagues did the work? No way. The first colleague (age eighteen) was curled up in the sun by the geraniums, his whiskers twitching in a feline dream. And the second (age two and new to the workforce) was alternately playing with my colored pens and chasing her gray bushy tail in the middle of my desk. As the saying goes, sometimes good help is hard to find. Remember that when you work at home, you may have to do it all.

Help aside, if you meet the above qualifications and are determined to join the ranks, by all means give it a go. I have colleagues who have worked at home for ages after making this important decision, swearing that they will work this way forever, till death do them part. And I know others who have tried it for a few years, then switched back to a company-based job because it felt right at that point. Either way, whether short-term or long-term, for those who wish to establish their own psychology of working at home, it can be an enriching workstyle. Go get your bathrobe and welcome to the club.

AVOCATION

FOR MANY people, the work they love best is what they do when the workday is over. That is, the activity they engage in *after* fulfilling their requisite hours at Company X or Ink, Inc., or Channel WORK or wherever they have their "regular" job. What I'm referring to, of course, is avocation.

Now I know that avocation has a bad rap. People don't take it seriously because it's done after hours. People think it isn't really work because, well, if a job isn't a person's actual livelihood, then what is the point? Well, rubbish on that, I say. And patoohey, too. Because the world is full of important work, both paid and unpaid—with more of it pro bono than we'll ever know. In fact, much of our greatest art, literature, music, philosophy, spiritual teaching, community service efforts, science and technology have been—and still are—produced through avocation.

Do you enjoy the poems of Wallace Stevens and William Carlos Williams, as I always do? These poets made their livings, respectively, as insurance salesman and pediatrician. Do you like to explore the philosophies of Plato and Nietzsche? Both of these influential philosophers—and a number of their colleagues—developed their theories while working as full-time educators.

Today, there is Zen master Charlotte Joko Beck, who studied and taught Zen for many years while supporting her family through the secretarial profession . . . Scott Adams, who created his famous *Dilbert* comic strip while he was a manager at Pacific Bell . . . and Lou Harrison, American gamelan composer, who has supplemented his musical income through a combination of "day jobs," including being a reporter, record salesman, forest fire-fighter, and animal nurse.

Think of Mother Teresa, who for decades ministered to the sick and poor on the streets of Calcutta. Mother Teresa who said, "We shouldn't be so concerned with doing great things as doing small things with great love." Think of the thousands of others who are doing just that: performing their true work not for money, but out of great love, a deep sense of caring, a passion for life and for art—in the name of avocation.

MANY AVOCATIONS, MANY POSSIBILITIES

There are so many possibilities, so many reasons, for avocation. Some people are drawn to helping others in third world countries, like Bonnie, a teacher I know who spends her summers building houses in remote villages of El Salvador. Some are dedicated to sharing their spiritual practice, like my Buddhist nun friend who teaches meditation classes in a Boston city jail. Many are fulfilling a creative passion, as with my New York cabdriver friend Nate, who writes off-Broadway plays in his noncabbing hours. Still others regard their avocation as pure relaxation: Henry, a district court judge and award-winning painter, spends leisurely weekends painting watercolors in his studio overlooking Santa Fe.

Some find that their avocation complements their vocation. For example, Davis, a computer technician, says he is driven toward his avocation—composing and playing Celtic music. Music chose him and that is that, is how he puts it; he doesn't have a whole lot of choice. But at the same time, he enjoys fulfillment in his full-time job. "Basically, I'm a whole-brain kind of cat," he explains. "Computers exercise the left side, music the right. The two keep me in balance."

When I first met Davis, this seemed literally to be the case. He had just gotten out of his car in the parking lot of a high-tech company where I was doing contract work, and he was carrying a toolbox in one hand and a guitar in the other. I noticed that his car sported one of those bumper stickers I had always liked: "Support the arts. Kiss a musician." Feeling impulsive that day (plus, let's face it, I liked the way he looked), I did just that: delivered a huge smacker to his right cheek. Grinning afterward, we introduced ourselves and shook hands. Then we got to the subject of avocation.

One thing I asked Davis was if he would play music full time if he had the chance. "Maybe some day," he shrugged. "But right now, I like my music where it is. When it isn't a regular gig, there are fewer complications. Without deadlines or pressure, I can take my time. I don't have to worry about someone else feeling I should perform a certain way. Without someone else's expectations haunting me, I can go deeper into my work."

Besides, he explained, his daytime job offers a lot of advantages. The technical work is a challenge, he earns a good salary, and he has plenty of creative energy left over. And his company has a great library where, on his breaks, he reads five international daily newspapers, surfs the Internet for music-related information, and studies Gaelic in anticipation of traveling to Ireland and Wales. After all that is said and done, he has evenings and weekends free to compose and perform: to do his own work.

As Davis says, what more could he want? He has a job he likes, he makes a great living, and he has his creative passion. In his mind, it is "the best of all possible worlds."

TEACHER JOBS AND AVOCATION AS UNDERSTUDY

Then there is Beth, a waitress and actress, who views her vocation as an important teacher for her avocation. Her waitress job is the serious training ground; her acting career is the understudy. She has even given this "teacher job" a name: Mrs. Munsie, after a kind but no-nonsense drama instructor she had in college, a woman who took Beth under her wing and made a huge difference in her life.

Since Beth eventually hopes to make acting a full-time career, she wants to learn whatever she can to help make that a possibility, to turn her avocation into vocation. Thus, when she leaves for the restaurant each morning, she thinks of herself as attending coaching class with Mrs. Munsie. She sets her mind to pay complete attention and learn as much as she can.

So far, Mrs. Munsie has been an exemplary teacher. For example, as Beth interacts with people all day, her diction and facial expressions get a lot of practice. Recalling meal orders improves her skill at memorizing lines. The customers, with their great variety of mannerisms, accents, body languages, and social skills, are wonderful for character observation and imitation. Plus she has numerous opportunities to pretend to be on the stage—especially when customers are rude and she has to act pleasant and kind.

Oh, sure, some days are tough, Beth says, just like with any job. Some days she would like to tell Mrs. Munsie to go for a deep, dark hike. But mostly, the situation is positive; it gives her energy for her true work. She appreciates Mrs. Munsie for being her own personal endowment to the arts.

VOCATION AS AVOCATION

Sometimes vocation is also a person's avocation. Geoff, a dentist I know, spends his weekends providing free dentistry at an inner city clinic. And Ian, a landscaper I recently met at a gardening center, donates his off-work hours to creating beautiful gardens in and around urban housing projects.

Similarly, though writing is mostly my vocation, when I dust off my Zen psychological suspense novel, *Indefinite Escapes*, it becomes my avocation. About a murderer who escapes from federal prison and is on the lam in my neighborhood (and in my neighbor's house), the novel is what I do when my "day job" is over.

At this point I'm just having fun, digging in the dirt of my mind, adding a little water to thicken the plot—the mud pie approach to writing. I muck around in the mess as long as I like, write sentences like "The murderer and the murderer's wife were desperadoes on vacation from silence" and "Speculation is fine, but somewhere within lurks the inevitable: fact." I take pure advantage of poetic license as I make a thought a character and allow ideas to amble dominolike along a forest path. I flood the house with wild rivers made of telephone rings. I travel into it far and wide. Because at this point *Indefinite Escapes* isn't about deadlines or editors or book reviews or livelihood. It's about going deep into myself and enjoying my exploration through the words.

Avocation is about love, passion, heart and soul. It's saying, "I'm going to do this" and actually *doing it*, no matter what. It's jumping into the deepest river, traveling to the farthest regions, and staying true to yourself along the way. Avocation is doing whatever it takes to keep your work alive.

The next time you meet someone who is practicing avocation, give him or her a kiss. Because this is one dedicated soul. He may be developing an invention that will radically change the world. She may be documenting a cultural transformation or working for peace in a way that is worthy of the Nobel Prize. These folks could be workaday saints like Mother Teresa for all you know. Or maybe they are just creating a piece of art that will make life a little more interesting, imaginative, and insightful for the rest of us to enjoy.

Whatever it is, they are listening to an inner voice, following their hearts, pursuing a passion, answering a higher calling, devoting themselves to a crucial cause. They are doing the work of the soul called avocation—some of the most important work of all.

GIVING BACK

ALBERT EINSTEIN said, "A hundred times every day I remind myself that my inner and outer life depend on the labors of other men, living and dead, and that I must exert myself in order to give, in the same measure as I have received."

Yes, I realize this is a very serious statement: heavier than the seven-league boots some of us walk to work in each morning and laden with guilt trips for those of us who tend to travel those unscenic routes. But the fact of the matter is that, well, it's true. And because we know we are all in this world together and because we know it's up to us to make it a better place, we can get out our human-sized measuring cups and begin the process of giving back.

Of course many of us are already doing this in a number of areas. We are digging yellow fin potatoes in the local food-share garden, listening deeply to a colleague's problem, or paying the toll of the car behind us on the turnpike as my cyber friend Badger often does. We are making great strides in medical research or publishing books on spiritual healing. And at the most basic level, as Dar likes to say, we are eating our carrots, so we can see more clearly what we need to do.

This reminds me of a charismatic newspaper publisher whose Christmas party I attended several years ago. I was at the hors d'oeuvres table, wearing something fancy and sipping a glass of something expensive, when someone interesting appeared and asked what I did for a living. Though this person didn't have an Italian accent and didn't strike me as someone I would converse with for the rest of my life, we did agree that the Gorgonzola fondue was out of this world. Then we moved on to some publishing shoptalk, which brought us to the topic of giving back.

I hadn't met the publisher before, but I often read her editorials. They were human-sized measuring-cup type of pieces, always with a different twist on ways to give to the world. That week her column had been about a quiet gesture she performed every morning on her commute to work: inviting cars to go ahead of her in rush-hour traffic. If I hadn't been paying attention, I would have missed it. I would have thought, "That's no new concept, I've done it myself countless times," and gone on to the next page. Even so, I continued to read.

The publisher and I discussed that column as we finished off the Gorgonzola fondue and the caterers replenished the dish. We talked of the twist she worked into that column: about how a simple gesture like letting someone into the traffic line takes you beyond the gesture itself. In doing so, you acknowledge the part of yourself that is capable of being open, of feeling how connected you are to everyone, no matter if they are isolated in their own rush-hour-bound cars. Of course, there are times when you might feel *too* connected, the publisher said, recalling the man who was so drop-dead gorgeous that she almost rear-ended him as he pulled into line. "It's a good thing an image of my husband suddenly popped into my head, or I might have had a full-blown accident on my hands," she said with a grin.

Allowing in the car in front of you is such a basic gesture. And yet it is so much more. It is an opening to be in touch with the depths of your own experience, to be more aware of what more you have to give every day. Which is an invitation to a more total act of giving. To make similar gestures in our workplaces . . . and to our families . . . and to our friends . . . and within our communities. And, within this framework, to find more opportunities for giving back. Let me count the ways. . . .

MENTORING

One way to give is to become a mentor. In Homer's *Odyssey*, Mentor was the faithful advisor who helped Odysseus to win the Trojan War; hence the meaning of the word today. Though the majority of us may not have a war to overcome, we can offer assistance to another in the spirit of being teacher, advisor, support system, and guiding light. We can give the benefits of our own experience.

You might do formal mentoring like Paul, a senior high-tech manager, who works with new hires in his company's mentoring program. Drawing on thirty-plus years of experience, he guides young software designers through everything from changes in technology to corporate protocol. Or you might tutor a sixth grader in math on Saturday mornings through an educational tutoring program, as Lee has been doing for several years. Or be a visiting artist in an inner-city community center, like my painter friend Nance.

Garth, a Black engineer I know, contacts high schools and meets informally with African American high school students, hoping to give them a head start in the working world. He frankly discusses growing up in the South, working his way through college, struggling with discrimination in various workplaces, and, at the age of forty-eight, earning a doctorate in computer science and netting a good position with a Fortune 500 company. He encourages them to attend college, to make life goals, to be proud contributors to the workforce. Then he follows up by passing out his card, in case anyone should need personal advice or ongoing support.

Why does he do it? "It's tough out there," he says. "If I can prevent one kid from going through the hard times I experienced, it will be worth all the time."

At some point you may become an accidental mentor such as when someone in your field chooses you. I am such a mentor, as I have a few writers who regularly seek me out for suggestions, editorial commentary, or a supportive ear. One of these people calls me "Coach." He telephones when he has questions, when he is elated, and when he has what he calls "the publishing blues." I try to listen completely in the way that other writers have listened to me in the past. Then I toss out my standard phrases: "Publishing is wonderful," "Publishing is hell," and "Go for it anyway." And I follow it all up with a few legacies passed along from my own mentors:

- "Make sure your work is really clean before you send it out."
- "Focus on a new project rather than halting all activity and pitching a pup tent by your mailbox to wait for the last manuscript to come back."
- "Appreciate your editors. These are the people who recommend adding the ginkgo-leaf scarf or the glittery belt to the good black dress that is your manuscript. They are the ones who make sure your sleeves aren't wrinkled and your slip isn't showing. And they always check to see that, in your excitement, you haven't dribbled Gorgonzola fondue down your front. They want you to look your very best. They are worth their weight in gold."

Often as I share these wisdoms, I remember that mentoring is also about mentoring yourself. Because, as the Roman philosopher Seneca said, you learn while you teach. You get in touch with what you know, with what you need to find out. You see more clearly your strengths and limitations. And you increase your awareness of where you have been in your career, and how far you have traveled—even if some days it feels like you have only been to the Ideal Market and back. Mentoring gives you a sense of where you are going and what you need to do in your own work to grow. So when you mentor, you are not only giving back to the world, you are giving to yourself as well.

GIVING BACK TO YOUR SUPPORTERS

Another way to give back is by acknowledging those who have supported you in your life and in your work. Appreciating the nights your assistant brought Burmese takeout to your desk when you were on the deadline from hell; the time an ex-colleague remembered you when she needed a copy writer for her catalog collection of Chilean arachnids; the folks in your life who routinely help your work to run more smoothly today—and considering what you might do for them in return.

If you are like me, your list of these people extends from here to Mars and probably includes a few Martian types, too. There are employers, colleagues, spouses, children, parents, friends, teachers, students, readers, and spiritual leaders. There is Carole, the writer who befriended me in high school and with whom I still correspond twenty-some years later; and Leni, the Russian artist who introduced me to Hermann Hesse and Ayn Rand and once rescued my favorite dress when the iron caught on fire. Not to forget my Great-Aunt Eleanore, who went out of her way to buy my last book, although she certainly didn't need to read about temporary employment at the age of ninety-seven. It's amazing, when you put your mind to it, how many people star on that list.

My friend Ann gives back to her ex-colleagues in Colorado by sending fresh almonds and flowers from her California garden. Peter often writes letters to employers, gives references, or takes a former boss to lunch. Once my colleague Sandie rewrote a résumé for a temporary staffing manager who had found many lucrative technical writing assignments for her before he decided to change fields. Although he offered to pay her standard fee, she was pleased to have the opportunity to do something for him in return.

One of my favorite stories in this category involves a lawyer whose wife heads up his list of supporters. Early in their marriage she delayed her own education to put him through law school. She helped him study for the bar and listened as he settled into his new firm. It was only after he was firmly established in his career that she returned to school to pursue her degree in art. Thirty years later, he still appreciates the sacrifices she made on his behalf. So every morning he takes a break from his successful law practice and faxes a love note to her studio or calls her to remind her that she is his most important partner. Every day for him is about giving back.

GIVING BACK TO THE GREATER COMMUNITY

There are so many choices for giving to the community. The possibilities really are myriad. Yes, from the alpha control center of your very own desk, you can push a few buttons, pull a few levers, ring some bells, blow some whistles, and *voilà!*—in no time you have given back. For instance, you might

- Have money automatically transferred weekly or monthly from your paycheck to a charitable organization or an agency that distributes donations to a number of nonprofit groups.
- Find out if your company has a matching grant program for community organizations, then apply. My friend Hope does this by having her company match her donations to her community Philharmonic.
- Collect food from your colleagues to donate to a local food bank.
- Collect used items from your colleagues to donate to a women's shelter, special children's program, or veterans' organization.
- Ask your coworkers to sponsor you on walkathons or bikea-thons to fund research for muscular dystrophy, cancer, or AIDS.
- Encourage your company to sponsor community project days when employees take a day to help repair project housing, maintain hiking trails, or adopt a community area for litter con-

trol. A biotech company I know does this on a biannual basis. The projects are scheduled for a weekday, and all employees who participate are paid their regular salary.

- Find out if your company compensates employees for volunteer work, then volunteer.
- Hold a white elephant sale at work with your colleagues' oldies but goodies, and donate the proceeds to charity.
- Find out if your company has office equipment or furniture it no longer needs, and donate it to a vocational school or community program.

Another way you might give back is to take your professional skills into the community like Valerie, who does pro bono accounting at a homeless shelter once a month, and Jay, a physical education teacher who volunteers as recreation coordinator for a teen center. I know several Native Americans who have taken this one step further by learning a trade or technology that would benefit their nations, then returning to the community to put their new skills to work.

These are just a few ideas. You probably have several of your own. Combined, there are so many opportunities for getting involved with community.

GIVING TO CHILDREN

We've all heard of Take Your Kids to Work Day, but what about giving children positive attitudes about livelihood right now? What about encouraging them so they will have a head start on meaningful employment—every day? When I talked to Hannah about this, she joked, "I give my kids purple dinosaur vitamins each morning so they will grow up strong. Does that count?" Absolutely, I thought. What better gift than one of health?

A friend of mine who is an educational social worker says if an underprivileged child has just one positive adult role model in his life, he can overcome many difficulties and enjoy personal success as he grows up. "Imagine," she told me, "the advantages we can offer, not just to the underprivileged, but to all children, with what we have to give. Imagine who they can be if we listen, show appreciation for who they are, and encourage them to explore their interests. And think about what we are doing for the future of the world when we give these things?"

I think we might also take them to work on occasion, as Hannah does, and support work-study and school-to-work programs, where older students divide their time between learning and earning. At the same time, we can show them that our work means a lot to us but is never more important than family and friends.

Besides working with their own kids, a number of my colleagues volunteer through organized after-school programs. One boss of mine disappeared one afternoon a week to hike or attend a baseball game with his "little brother." My friend Burk, who still remembers many of the coaches from his youth, has for years coached elementary school softball and hockey. And I often "listen" to teens whom I meet in chat rooms on the Internet. They send me messages about practically everything going on in their lives, sometimes asking for advice, but mostly wanting to "talk" with someone who cares. I not only feel like I am giving back by offering an adult connection, but I often learn things that I can apply to my own life as well.

MINDFUL ACTION

I always try to remind myself that I can give back by practicing mindful action. By remembering that just about everything I do, everywhere I go, is someone's workplace—the bus or subway, the grocery store, the library, the busy intersection where street repairs are being made—and considering how my actions (or inactions) affect the people there. How I am in their workplace and what I say and do might make a difference to their work.

Once I was having dinner at a busy restaurant when the waitress stopped by—not to bring more food but to thank me for taking my time. Surprised, I said, "Isn't that what dinner is all about?" "Oh, no," she replied. She went on to explain that a lot of people are in a rush, requiring quick service, being impatient when everything doesn't happen on demand. Wanting to finish the business of eating so they can get on with the rest of their lives. All making this waitress's job hectic and often stressful. But when people took their time, her work was more pleasant and relaxed. It hadn't occurred to me that by wanting a leisurely meal, I was contributing to someone's positive work experience. That I was giving back.

An editor of mine had a similar experience. She told me that she used to smoke, and at the end of every day she would pour the contents of her ashtray into the wastebasket. One evening she was working late when the janitor came into her office to empty the basket. As she watched, she was horrified to see the ashes fly up from the basket and into his face—something she had never considered. After that, she was careful to contain the ashes in a plastic bag before placing them in the basket. And she thought more about the "invisible" employees—the people in her office who cleaned, shoveled snow, made repairs, did other important jobs behind the scenes—and what more she could do for them in mindful action. In the sense of giving back.

Sometimes someone else's work experience comes to us, such as when a magazine salesperson knocks on our door or a telemarketer phones. Although we may not welcome these intrusions into our lives or wish to buy their products, we can support the fact that these people are making efforts similar to our own. We can be pleasant and kind. In our minds, we can step outside that door and think about what it might feel like to be standing on that porch in the dark and the cold, all in the name of trying to make an honest livelihood. A turning point for me in this area came when my friend Tina, who had an excellent ESL background, took a telemarketing position when she couldn't find work in her field. Now, whenever I receive an unsolicited call, I think, This person is only trying to make a living, just like Tina. He is only trying to survive, just like me.

———————

Some days this may be the best thing we have to give: being kind to a magazine salesperson on the phone. Or thinking about how our ashes might fly into someone's face. Or allowing someone in traffic ahead of us in line. Some days it is being your very best self in the presence of others, like my friend Nick, to whom a colleague once said, "You are so comfortable in your world, so confident, so present. Being around you makes me feel good to be alive."

Some days giving back may be about an appreciation of the simple good things in our lives, like my friend who says of every glass of water she drinks, "This is the best glass of water I ever had." She isn't joking. She really means it. And it always strikes me, that moment of pure contact when that cold water reaches her mouth, because in appreciating that one sip you appreciate the whole world and everything in it. And with this connection, your life becomes an effort of giving back.

GROWING BEYOND
YOUR WORK

THERE IS one last thing I want to say. It is about work and endings. Naturally, I am thinking of this as I near the end of this book, which has taken me three years to write. It has been a long journey, a pilgrimage of sorts, as any long-term project often is. Now I am assailed with a million questions. Which of the myriad possibilities will present themselves as I move on to my next project? Where will they take me as I navigate my way along another work road? What characters will I meet in my elevator? What mountains will I climb? Will my new situation have a view?

As I entertain these questions, the temptation is to walk away before I am finished here. To put in a spot appearance for a paragraph or two, then roar off in search of the next possibility and leave you, dear reader, to determine the end for yourself. I know it sounds radical, but would that really be so bad? After all, no matter what wonderful wisdoms the employment gods bestow, we all must find the ending that works for us. Certainly, we can learn from the wisdoms that came before us. But ultimately we are the ones to carry on.

Oh, I know I have to finish the chapter, to complete this work, although I did once read a book called *Mount Analogue*, which ended not only in the middle of a sentence but with a comma. The author, René Daumal, had a good excuse for this, since he died during the writing (at the time I thought it was the best case of comma-tose I had ever heard). But most of us don't die before our work is over, even if it sometimes feels as though we might. We have to fulfill our contract, finish our work shift, tidy up the last sentence, and end it with a definite period before we move on. We have to fully conclude the book, the project, whatever it is, in the best possible way we can—not just to meet an obligation or to reach the top of the mountain, but to take the pilgrimage to the end. To meet the deep place within ourselves that knows we can do it, yes we can. To meet the place that connects us through our work to the rest of the world.

You might wonder, "If the beginning is the most important part of the work, is the ending the least important?" That is a very good question. I suppose logic would follow that if the beginning is the most momentous aspect of our work, an ending would have less significance. But the thing about endings is that they are beginnings, too, for as they complete one cycle they start the next. They point to an entertainment of the next round of possibilities. In our lives and in our work, we are on continuous cycles. We are always beginning, ending, and beginning again.

John Steinbeck said, "Man, unlike any other thing organic or inorganic in the universe, grows beyond his work, walks up the stairs of his concepts, emerges ahead of his accomplishments." When I first read this, I fell wildly in love with this combination of words. Because they point to so many options. Because they evoke a strong sense of the human race moving forward, pulling individuals along. Except that we aren't actually being pulled. No, we are walking upward and outward of our own accord, making life happen with every step. Even if it sometimes feels that we are going nowhere, we are the ones climbing the mountain. We are emerging ahead of our accomplishments, ahead of ourselves.

Think you're stuck? I can relate to that. This happened to me when I was writing this book. For the longest time I slid back down the mountain; it didn't seem possible that I would ever move forward again. I wrote whole drafts that reincarnated upon completion, and rewrote those drafts again. I wrestled with the sudden fierce animals of my fears, my limitations, as thousands of vultures flapped overhead. All of this was a surprise for me. I was accustomed to having my work go well, whether it was writing or another project. I was used to producing pieces of writing magically through what I thought of as my personal brand of "abracadeborah." I wasn't used to being unable to count on myself. Worker's block was the bane of someone else's existence, not mine.

Valerie quietly suggested that maybe I hadn't really been writing before, that I hadn't seriously tested my depths. She said maybe I hadn't been growing *in* my work, so how could I grow beyond it? While she offered undying support, she saw my struggle as a teaching, an opportunity to unload the terrific burden of my ego that was so attached to events unfolding in a particular way. She also saw this as a time for me to set work aside to care for the important personal areas of my life that needed attention. She saw all of this as me growing beyond my work.

At that point, I didn't want to think about lessons or growth. I wanted to avoid the difficulties and get on to the next project as quickly as possible. But after I finished hating Valerie's guts for her valuable insights, I had to admit she was right. So I dug in my heels, killed a few thousand more words, and recommenced my climb.

I am reminded here of a story I heard about a monk living in a temple in Japan. The monk was *tenzo*, the person who cooks all the meals for everyone in the temple—day after day, year after year. When asked what he liked about this work, he replied that he found joy in preparing something well today that he hadn't prepared so well the day before. I was really struck by that. It also occurred to me that I could apply this principle to my own work, whether I was writing a book, teaching a class, editing a magazine article, or stuffing envelopes. By concentrating on my abilities, paying attention to my efforts day by day, I could prepare my work better than I had the day before. I could continue to learn.

Another part of growing involves how you choose to view the world. This has become abundantly clear to me over the past few years as I spend time with a close friend who has Alzheimer's disease—as I watch the disease take away pieces of her life. Athough she is only in her fifties, she can no longer do her photography work or teach yoga. She doesn't remember how to drive her car, and the simple task of counting change completely eludes her. Yet, with the help of her friend and caregiver, she has taken up painting and discovered new ways to plant her garden. Even with Alzheimer's, she is growing beyond her work.

We walk together every Sunday. Often we talk about how long it might be before her awareness slips away. Other times we speculate about what will happen when she dies. Sometimes she cries, wishing she had more time. Still, she pushes to work with what she has. Invariably, every week, she looks up at the mountains and says, "Aren't we lucky to be here?" And I have to agree that we are.

Bibliography

Dalai Lama, *A Policy of Kindness: An Anthology of Writings by and about the Dalai Lama* (Ithaca, NY: Snow Lion, 1990).

Daumal, René, *Mount Analogue* (Boston: Shambhala, 1986).

Dominguez, Joe, and Vicky Robin, *Your Money or Your Life: Transforming Your Relationship with Money and Achieving Financial Independence* (New York: Viking Penguin, 1992).

Elgin, Duane, *Voluntary Simplicity: Toward a Way of Life That Is Outwardly Simple, Inwardly Rich* (New York: William Morrow, 1993).

Suzuki, Shunryu, *Zen Mind, Beginner's Mind* (New York & Tokyo: Weatherhill, 1970).

Trungpa, Chögyam, *Shambhala: The Sacred Path of the Warrior* (Boston & London: Shambhala, 1984).

Weil, Simone, *Gravity and Grace* (London: Routledge & Keegan Paul, 1952).

Wing, R. L., *The Illustrated I Ching* (New York: Doubleday, 1982).